# Peer Praise For Jackson's Debut Novel

"When wildfires break out and rage through the Everglades, destroying natural habitat and creeping close to homes, folks around Cypress City suspect somebody's lighting them. Ben Gates believes he's the man to find the arsonist. Trouble is, folks also think he might be the culprit. And so Tim Jackson's intelligent thriller gets a jump start into its wild and vivid exploration of the vicious conflicts in Southwest Florida between various vested interests in using or abusing the land. The story pits eco-activists against developers in a complicated entanglement that involves the Park Service, the National Guard, and a collection of long-time residents with long-term grudges against one another. Plotted with the intricate complexity of a *Chinatown*, Jackson's novel boasts a gritty authenticity coupled with literary mastery to achieve a thoroughly believable, vivid portrait of a place writhing in the grip of change."

> - C .W. Smith, author of nine novels, including *Buffalo Nickel, Understanding Women, he Vestal Virgin Room* and the forthcoming *Steplings*.

"*Mangrove Underground* is an ambitious portrait of a rapidly changing land. In Jackson's prose, the Florida backcountry becomes a chaacter itself, as fully engaged as, and evolving through, the story as any of its people. It's a beautifully-written novel that never fails to entertain."

> - Robert R Bowie Jr., author of *There Ain't No Wyoming, Naked House Painting Society* and *Sonnets*.

"The only thing as riveting as Tim's powerful storytelling with *Mangrove Underground* is the depth and intrigue of the stories he tells. Pick a plot - any plot - in this fast-paced adventure and you find compelling dialogue, intrigue, characters and vulnerabilities all wrapped up with incredible opportunities for redemption and resolution. Blend a handful of these mesmerizing vignettes together - brilliantly intertwined in a way that rises and falls as dramatically and subtly as the tides Tim navigates. What results is page-turning, marsh-burning thriller from a marvelous new voice in literature."

> - James Dale, author of *IF GOD STOPS WORKING: Rethinking Religion to Find a Faith That's Real*.

# MANGROVE UNDERGROUND

Tim W. Jackson

The Chenault Publishing Group, LLC

MANGROVE UNDERGROUND
Tim W. Jackson

http://www.timwjackson.com

Published by:

The Chenault Publishing Group, LLC
120 S. Denton Tap, Suite 450
Box 121
Coppell, Texas 75019

10 9 8 7 6 5 4 3 2 1

First Edition © 2011 by Tim W. Jackson

This is a work of fiction. Names, characters, places and incidents are either the
product of the author's imagination or are used fictitiously. Any resemblance
to actual persons, living or dead, business establishments, events or locales is
entirely coincidental. The publisher does not have any control over and does
not assume any responsibility for author or third-party websites or their content.

Hardcover ISBN: 978-0-9825626-6-6
Softcover ISBN: 978-0-9825626-7-3
Ebooks ISBN: 978-0-9825626-9-7

The Library of Congress Control Numbers applied for.

Cover concept and illustration by Marylee Boarman.
Design and production by Jay Zwerner.
Edited by Kay Russo

Printed in the United States of America

*To my parents,*
*Charlie and Janice Jackson,*
*and to my wife Jana, the true believers.*

# Acknowledgements

Thanks to the many people who helped breathe life into this book
on its long, strange trip to publication.

C.W. Smith and the Southern Methodist University
graduate writing program for the beginning, Bob Bowie for the ending,
and the many patient readers in-between who slogged through drafts
and offered comments, advice and encouragement:

## On Little Cayman
Julie Cherry
Cornelia Olivier
Ann Walther

## In Dallas
Jana VanAntwerp
Charlie and Marcie Waskey

Thanks also to the Brooksville (Fla.) Fire Department
and the Florida Division of Forestry for letting an aspiring photojournalist
tag along and ask questions on countless wildfires way back in the 1990s.

Special thanks to Kay Russo for her professional editing
and for walking me through the stylistic transition from
Associated Press to Chicago Manual of Style.

The Frosty Gator in Idaho Falls is real and once provided this thin-blooded
Southerner a welcome refuge on a blustery winter evening.
My thanks for that as well.

*"It is good to have
an end to journey towards;
but it is the journey that
matters in the end."*

- *Ursula K. Le Guin*

1

And then, after paddling daylong among the over-grown Calusa shell-mounds, they reached the Dogwater ground site. The river shone dull orange with the setting sun. In the lead canoe, James Gates raised his paddle, a racer crossing the finish line, a silhouette suspended in the wisps of fog rising from the water. The boy dug his paddle deep, letting the brackish water cool his hands. The canoe angled left as his mother ruddered them closer to shore.

The Park Service dock, even with the top of the riverbank, loomed five feet above Ben's head. Low tide. He reached for the nearest piling, and then pulled back as clumps of mud scuttled away from his hand. More fiddler crabs scurried across the undersides of the planks above. Ben leaned away as far as he could.

"Come on, Son. Time's a-wasting!" His father's head and shoulders appeared above him.

A wooden ramp sloped up at the end of the dock, its planks coated in mud. Ben eased a foot onto the ramp, slipped and landed on his knees. Leaning on his paddle, he pulled himself up the mud-slicked wood slat-by-slat.

James Gates grabbed Ben's arm and pulled him to the top of the bank. "Damn, son. You got more swamp on you than around you."

Beyond the dock the mangrove wall opened into a clearing big enough for several tents. In the center sat a weathered picnic table. James Gates' hand was warm and heavy on Ben's shoulder.

"We get us a fire going, this'll feel like home."

"I could use some help here!" Beth Gates' voice drifted from the dock.

Ben's dad winked at him. "Yankees," he said. Ben smiled, knowing what was coming.

"What are you two whispering about up there?"

"About how city folks are always in a hurry," James Gates called back. "Never taking time to relax, enjoy life."

"Same people who go hungry because they're too busy relaxing to unload the food?"

"Us swamp men are busy up here. Chasing off panthers and bears and skunk apes." He winked at Ben again. "Start on that tent, son. We'll be back directly."

The mangroves crowded twice Ben's height around the campsite. His parents' voices drifted through the clearing, pushing back the gathering fog. He unrolled the tent by the picnic table, its entrance flap facing the water. More fog rolled up from the river, nuzzling through the mangrove limbs. On the dock, his parents were dark forms in the thickening air, lifting boxes and duffel bags from the canoes. Something rustled in the mangroves to his right, then to his left. Ben froze, wide-eyed, expecting yellow panther eyes staring back at him, or charging bears.

"This fog can be kind of spooky, can't it?" His mom set a small ice chest on the table.

"No. Are there really bears here?"

"Your father's just playing with you." She knelt so her eyes were level with his. "There are bears in the swamp. It's their home, and we're the visitors. But with us making this much noise, they're a long way from here."

"There's things... watching us."

She slid an arm around his shoulders. "You mean the Nunnehi."

Ben spun, expecting dark shapes to spring from the fog.

"It's OK," she laughed. "The Calusas said spirit people – the Nunnehi – lived out here. They looked after hunters and travelers, kept them safe, guided them back to their homes." She smoothed his hair, eased him back down. "All these clearings we camp in? They're Nunnehi Rings – the safest places in the swamp. You're pretty sharp. You feel them checking on us, making sure we're all right."

Ben shivered despite the humid air. He didn't believe her, but he didn't want her to stop talking. Or to know he was worried by the swamp sounds.

"There was a boy who got lost near here once. About 10 years old." She squeezed his shoulders to make sure he was listening. "He'd been out fishing, went too far and fell asleep in his boat. Sound familiar?"

He shrugged, intent on the rustlings beyond in the brush. He wasn't afraid. And wouldn't be.

"Well, when he woke it was dark and foggy. Just like this. You can imagine how... nervous he was. After a few minutes he heard noises. Voices. People to help him find his way. He didn't want the other people to know he was nervous, so instead of calling out, he paddled his skiff toward them. The people moved away, always just beyond where he could see. He followed for what felt like forever, through all sorts of twists and turns and side channels, deep among the mounds, until his arms were numb and he felt he couldn't paddle anymore.

"He was about to give up when he saw the yellowy glow of a campfire. He steered his skiff to shore and found himself in a clearing – this clearing – where a group of people were camped. Their clothes and gear were strange, like the old-time re-enactors we saw that time, but he was so happy to finally find people he didn't pay much attention. They gave him hot chocolate and some stew and let him stay in their big tent that night. In the morning the boy woke with the sun bright on his face. The tent, the people, the fire pit, everything was gone except his canoe. That's when he realized there had been no other boats on the shore the night before, even though a boat's the only way to get here.

"Can you imagine how nervous he was then? He raced home as fast as he could, not daring to tell his parents what had happened, afraid they would think he was crazy or making it up."

Ben's eyes were bright, seeing pavilion tents and magical lights sprouting around him.

"You're lucky," his mom said. "Most people never realize the Nunnehi are out here. They're too busy to trust their feelings or really respect the wilderness." She smoothed his hair again. "The Nunnehi will watch over us all night."

"And grab you while you sleep!"

Ben jumped at his dad's growl.

"James, you're not helping," his mom laughed. "Your father doesn't believe anything he can't see."

"Fog's just fog," his dad said. "Anything in the bushes looking at me better be careful. I might look back."

"He grew up out here, but there's still things he can't see," Beth Gates said as she smiled and looked past Ben, toward his dad.

"I want religion, I'll go to church," James Gates replied with his own grin. "The swamp was here long before tree huggers came along to make it warm and fuzzy." He tapped the side of his head and raised his eyebrows. "That's what college does to you, Boy. Remember that."

Ben only half-heard them. He peered into the fog, eager for any movement, not believing the story, but wanting to.

After dinner by the fire, Ben followed his dad to the dock. The foggy air felt thick in his lungs. Away from the fire, he could have been walking through a cloud, the dirt beneath his boots the only thing solid. Then broad planks appeared at his feet. The dock. Four more steps and they were at the corner, where the L-shaped dock turned and ran

5

parallel with the river. His dad squatted and checked the lines holding the canoes.

Frogs screeched below the dock, in the trees behind, and across the river. Mosquitoes buzzed. Down the shore something cried out, a low keening at water level.

"Night heron," his dad murmured.

Metal clanked at the far end of the dock, near the ramp down to the river. A globe of dim yellow light floated at ground level, and then disappeared below. His mom, going to scrub the aluminum plates and pans. More clanking, water splashed, and his mom's humming floated up through the fog.

"Nothing out here that don't belong," his father spoke quietly. "Fog, frogs, gators. You, if you're lucky. Trick is figuring where you fit in. Or letting the swamp show you."

Ben squatted, copying his father. The fog pressed the sounds and smells close around him. The reek of mud filled him, coated him.

"You listen, let everything settle around you," his dad said. "Get to a point, you feel like the swamp accepts you, and you go quiet and careful then, not wanting to spoil that."

Neither spoke for several minutes. Ben picked out new sounds around him. Tree frogs chirping at a higher pitch than those under the dock. Something small, mousy, moving in the brush behind him. Metallic scraping as his mom scrubbed at the dried cheese in the big stew pot. Canoes thumping softly against the pilings below. Upriver and midstream, something like steam escaping a vent, quickly shut off, then a splash of something slipping into the water. The sound repeated, then two, four, five times all at once, moving toward the dock.

"Dolphins," his dad whispered. "Six, maybe seven. Tide's bringing out all kinds of little fish for them."

Ben strained to see through the fog as the sounds drew even with the dock then passed on. "How'd they get here?"

"The Gulf's only a few miles downstream. Remember?"

He squatted, stock-still, listening for the whispers of spirit people, anything more than the night breeze among unseen tree limbs, the scrape of pans. He breathed lightly so as not to disturb anything around him, safe between his parents.

His mom yelled. Pans clattered at the base of the ramp. She yelled again, louder. His dad was running down the dock before Ben could move. She screamed, her voice finally forming a word.

"James!"

When Ben reached the end of the dock, his dad was pulling her up the ramp. Her right arm was tucked to her chest, her left hand locked on her wrist.

"It looked like a stick the current washed up," she said. "I pushed it away, and it bit me!"

"What kind?" His dad shooed him back.

"The black kind! The biting kind!"

"Ben! The med kit! Go!"

Ben ran for the campsite, his father's heavy footsteps behind him, carrying his mother back.

By the time Ben found the first aid kit, his mother was lying on the table, his father hunched over her. His dad snatched at the kit from him and dug for the snakebite kit. His mom yelled as his dad cut her hand. Dark blood oozed where the knife touched her skin. Ben turned away. This wasn't his mom. Not helpless and screaming like this. He shut his eyes as tight as he could. She would be fine. It was just a snake.

His dad bandaged her hand and helped her into the tent, then crawled back out.

"She'll be fine. A little sore, but..." Ben had never heard his dad's voice shake like this. His dad stared into the fog, eyes unfocused. "She'll be fine... We need a doctor."

Ben jumped up, grabbed a paddle.

"Whoa, son! Think, then act." His dad spread a chart across the table and tapped a black tepee-shape near the top edge. "We're here. Dogwater ground site. Nearest help we know of is Silver Bay research hut. Should at least be a radio there." His finger tapped a patch of blue two chart folds away. Ben listened, but knew his dad was talking to himself. "Six, maybe eight hours' hard paddling. In the morning. We miss a turn at night... We can't waste time. We won't waste time." He leaned on the chart, like he was holding it down in a stiff wind. "High tide, the best way's here, through the Tangles."

"Tangles?"

"It's real narrow. And shallow." His finger zigzagged across the map, following a thin blue squiggle winding south through the green of mangroves. "Comes out here. Tarpon River. Then straight up to Silver Bay. No time to run down to the Gulf and back up."

"When's high tide?"

"Dunno. Need a tide chart."

"What's that?"

Remember that piece of paper with the river names and all the numbers? The one you set on the bags yesterday that the wind blew away?"

Ben felt sick. He looked away, into the fog, squeezed his arms tight across his ribs. "Are there snakes? In the Tangles?"

His dad laid a hand on the boy's shoulder. "We'll do alright. Lord willing and the tide cooperates."

His mom moaned then, and his dad ducked into the tent. Ben stuffed gear into duffle bags as fast as he could. He heard his mom's voice quiet, strained.

"You and Ben are going to paddle us all that way?"

"Well, I don't know about Ben." A forced laugh from his dad. "'Reckon he can set in the bow and shove branches out of the way."

The fog closed in around Ben at that. His parents' voices blended into the hum of mosquitoes and frogs. He was useless. No. He could have everything packed, ready to go in the morning. The cooking box sat open beside him. Something cold slid down his back. The cook kit was still at the river. Ben climbed onto the table, watching the gray swirls that hid the river. He would leave them for his dad to get – the last thing they tossed in the canoe as they cast off. With all the fog, he wasn't even sure where the dock was.

'*We can't waste time,*' his dad had said.

He could miss the dock completely, fall down the riverbank. And if he did find the dock, the ramp was still slick. It was dangerous to try. Ben wanted to swallow, but his mouth was too dry.

'*I don't know about Ben,*' echoed through his head. He could do more than shove branches. '*We can't waste time.*' Ben grabbed a flashlight and a paddle, stepped with numb legs toward the river.

"Nunnehi?" he whispered. His mom's story came fresh into his head. He felt foolish calling out, but if there really were spirit people, his mom needed them. Nothing moved in the fog, but he felt stronger as he said the word. "Nunnehiiii," he said louder.

Ben stepped through the mangroves, holding the paddle in front of him. The mud smell hit him then, as if the swamp had exhaled in his face. His breathing drowned out the frogs. The packed mud in the milky oval of the flash-light was all he could see as he counted off ten, a dozen shuffle-steps.

Then, at his feet, there were boards sloping to the river. He shone the light down the ramp. The water had risen, swirling black around the pilings. His light glinted off three aluminum pots at the water's edge.

Ben looked behind him, hoping to see his dad, or a ghostly Nunnehi. There was only the campfire's yellow glow.

They didn't need the pans. If the water kept rising, it would wash them away. A snake could be anywhere down there. Under the ramp. Coiled in the mangrove roots. Curled around a pot so it looked like a shadow. He could tell his dad... No. He couldn't.

He reached the paddle as far as he could and tapped the boards. There was a hollow thump, but nothing moved. He hit the ramp again, harder. The boards boomed. He hit them again and again until he felt the vibration in the hard mud under his feet and heard the pots rattle at the water. Still nothing moved.

Holding his breath, he edged down the ramp sideways, holding the paddle like a machete. He dug the edges of his boots into the slick mud, whispering, "Nunnehi, Nunnehi," with each step. The air cooled as he neared the water. Ben reached with the paddle and slid the pots and plates up the ramp one at a time. He pressed them against his chest to stop them from rattling, then scrambled up the ramp and ran for the campfire.

At the camp, Ben climbed on the table again and closed his eyes, trying to stop shaking. From the tent he could hear his mom's voice, but not her words. His dad kept saying, "You'll be alright, Beth. You'll be alright."

A scuffling noise, footsteps, woke Ben. The fog was brighter. Somewhere above the white glow an osprey cried.

"Come on, son. Time's a-wasting." James Gates' eyes were dark, like he'd been hit. He had an arm around Ben's mom, walking her to the river. She looked half asleep, her face stretched and pale.

11

"Hey, Ben," she whispered. "You get things cleaned up?"

"Ma'am?"

"Packed up, I mean?" She held her hand across her chest. He choked and stepped back. Her hand had been replaced with something black and puffy, like an inflated rubber glove stuck on her arm. Knuckles and wrist bones had all been swallowed under skin stretched tight up to her elbow.

"Ben?" His dad's voice was too high. "I need you to hold the canoe steady while we get her situated. You do that?"

Ben ran for the river. He stumbled on a root, caught himself. The jolt cleared his mind. His mom was hurt. If they failed... He had to help his dad, help his mom.

His dad had rigged one canoe with a domed covering of branches and a blue poncho, a sleeping bag spread beneath it. Ben glanced at the mangrove roots snaking through the water, and then pulled the canoe to the ramp. His mom pressed something into his hand as he helped ease her into the canoe.

"You're the navigator, Ben. This'll help you find your way."

Ben stared at the Silva compass she used to guide them through the backcountry every trip. He nodded, and then climbed into the bow, setting the compass on his knee as he'd seen his mother do so often. He would get them through. It was his duty now.

The canoe rolled slightly as they pushed off.

The mangrove shoreline faded into the fog. In a few seconds Ben could barely see individual trees. They kept close to shore, the bank a dark smudge to their left. Southwest, the compass read. Ben dug his paddle into the river and listened to the water gurgle on either side of the bow. He leaned forward until he couldn't see the canoe, as if they were flying, making up for time lost.

A dark post loomed to the left. Then Ben saw the orange reflectors and the red-bordered triangle of the channel marker nailed to its top.

"Heads up, son." It could have been one word. "Watch for more markers." The canoe cut toward the post.

The shore parted as they neared, separated into trees on either side, and they were off the Dogwater and into a wide creek. The creek split, and they edged toward a vague channel marker near the right fork. Roots and fallen branches crowded in, sticking up from the water, scraping the canoe. Branches arched overhead, dripping dew. They had to slow as the branches hung lower, thicker. Wet leaves brushed Ben's arms. There was a scraping sound, and he turned to see the branch-and-poncho canopy slide over his dad's head and fall behind the canoe.

"Go, Ben! Go!" His dad yelled.

"James!" his mom whispered. "He's doing everything he can. You both are."

Ben tried to look away from her but couldn't.

"Paddle!" His dad was a stranger, eyes so dark, face so drawn. His dad was scared. Only his dad didn't get scared. Ben looked at his mom lying with her eyes closed.

His paddle shook, clattering on the gunwales.

"Ben!" His dad's murmur was loud in the still air. "We need to get through this creek quick like the bunny, without hurting your mama, alright?"

Ben dug his paddle deep. The blade caught on the creek bottom, and he dragged the canoe forward, like he did when exploring the shallow creeks near town with his friends Henry and Bailey. Only this was real. He wished Henry were here. Henry never got scared.

Soon he was grabbing branches and pulling them along. Twice they climbed out to float the canoe over downed trees. He cringed at his mom's moans when they bumped against unavoidable branches.

The fog swirled through the brush, rising in slender shapes that evaporated when Ben looked too close. He imagined the shapes were Nunnehi guiding him through the Tangles. He whispered so only he could hear, asking them to help. The shapes clustered thicker ahead, and he paddled harder, trying to catch up. He was sure they were waving, calling him on. That was crazy, he knew, but it made him feel better.

Soon the fog gave way to a deep green-and-yellow haze as the sun climbed higher somewhere above the trees. Whether because of the spirit people or not, Ben could see farther upstream. The water deepened. They came around a narrow turn, and he barely had time to duck before they plowed into a wall of mangrove limbs. Branches clawed at his arms and shoulders. Then the branches were gone.

He looked up, then covered his eyes from the bright sun. The canoe sat in a small lake, maybe fifty yards wide.

Ben sat blinking. The heat soaked in, pushing away his fears. They were through. Behind him, his dad was blinking, too, paddle across his knees, body heaving with every breath. His mom could have been asleep, but her face was splotched with red and her lips were dark, cracked. His dad laid a palm across her forehead.

"Where's the station?"

"Miles yet, Bubba." His dad's face looked splotchy as his mom's. "Tarpon River's still a half-mile that way."

Ben paddled. In moments they were winding down a wide creek. The sun and the glare from the water stabbed at his eyes, but that was okay. They were out of the Tangles. His mom's compass said they were headed due east. He whispered a thank-you to the Nunnehi.

The creek widened. After a broad turn, the mangroves fell away, and the creek flowed into a river wider than they had seen in days. Across the river a camping platform – a chickee – sat close in among the mangroves.

The river's current swung the canoe hard right. The tan creek water swirled with the dark brown river. They lurched back to the left, and Ben heard his dad's paddle splashing faster.

"Kick it, son!" he yelled.

Ben paddled as hard as he could, his arms and shoulders aching. The canoe crept across the current until they were even with the chickee, then beside it.

Ben jumped up to the platform, bow line in hand, and stopped. All he could see was river and more mangroves. His dad lay back in the canoe, eyes closed, chest heaving. His mom's face was still, waxy.

"This is it?" he said.

"Tarpon River chickee, Ben. Silver Bay's five miles that way." His dad pointed upriver.

"But the water's going the wrong way... "

"If someone hadn't lost the damn tide chart!" His dad sat up, glanced at the piling next to him. "High water's . . . Hell! The sumbitch just turned! Six hours before it slacks."

"So we can rest?"

"No!" His dad leaned forward and put his hands on his wife's cheeks. "Burning up," he whispered. "Sorry, Beth. Hell of a streak. Snake, night, fog, now tide." He leaned forward, head in his hands.

Ben grabbed at a corner post to steady himself. They were as bad off as ever. No shadow-shapes motioned from the trees or rose from the water. It wasn't his fault. The tide would still be going out even if he hadn't lost the tide chart.

The food bag and a canteen thumped at his feet. "Grab some chow. Stoke up for the home stretch." His dad slapped Ben's leg. "We gonna do this, tide or no."

Ben choked down a few sticks of jerky and a Hershey bar without tasting them. He dropped the bag and canteen beside his dad and climbed back into the canoe, set his mom's compass on his knee. North-northeast.

His hands stung as he pushed off. Blisters from paddling so hard. That made him feel better. The current spun them downriver, but they straightened and forced their way upstream. Pain cut across his shoulders and down his arms. He clenched his teeth and paddled harder. If he hurt, that meant he was doing some good. His dad could fall apart, but he wouldn't. He didn't need his dad, or the Nunnehi. Neither had brought them to safety yet. Neither had protected his mom in the first place. He could save her himself. All he had to do was paddle.

"Pace yourself, son!"

Ben ignored him. The water cooled his stinging palms. He switched sides to ease the burning in his shoulders. The mangrove thickets crept past. He watched the broad stretch of river in front of him, imagining a finish line at the horizon that he had to pull them past.

"You don't slow down, you'll waste yourself before we get there."

Ben kept paddling. He didn't need anyone. He would get them to the research hut before the tide changed. The canoe lurched forward as his dad paddled in time with him, following Ben's lead. He knew nothing but the splash of his paddle, the rush of water past the bow, the ache in his hands, knees, and shoulders. After a while he didn't bother to look past the brown water directly in front of him. Pull, reach and pull again. His arms were heavy. He didn't care.

"Ben. Hey! Ben!" Ben kept paddling. "Ben, grab that snag, you hear?"

A dead trunk, sun-bleached, jutted into the river just ahead. Ben lowered his head and pulled two, three, four times. The branch was only a few feet closer. He pulled three more times. The branch hadn't moved. He switched sides and paddled as hard as he could.

The world spun. He pulled again and the canoe jumped forward. Where the dead branch had been was nothing but brown water. The shore was 60, 70 yards away, like they'd crossed the river. A yellow leaf swirled past him, racing ahead in the current. He spun to his left. The mangroves were so close he could nearly touch them. South-southwest.

"No!"

"We got no juice left, Ben."

Ben grabbed at branches. His dad ruddered them away from shore. "We need to rest for when the tide eases."

"I can do it!"

"Ben! This ain't to make ourselves feel better. Anything not good for your mama, it's crap!"

Ben slumped forward, pressed his chest to his knees, trying to block out everything. His dad had quit. If his mom ... it was his dad's fault. He had been scared. He made them wait the night before. He made them stop now. They could have been in Silver Bay before the tide changed.

"Ben, if flat-out paddling would help, we'd have been there last night." His dad's voice was soft. "We're beat. For now." Ben covered his ears. This wasn't his dad. He saw the bleached trunk, as clear as if it were still in front of him. Only the harder he reached for it, the farther away it was.

He breathed deep, was surprised at a rasping sound in his chest. His face felt wet. He wouldn't let his dad see him like that.

The canoe bumped against something. The chickee. Ben steadied the canoe while his dad lifted his mom onto the platform.

"We gotta get you some shade, Beth."

She looked through him, through Ben. Then her eyes focused. "Hey, Ben. I heard you and the Nunnehi. They were talking to you, anyway." She put her good hand on his knee. "You listen for them. Trust them, even if they don't make sense."

Ben looked away as his dad set her in the shade. She rested in his dad's arms, sipping water from a canteen. Water trickled from the corners of her mouth.

"I'm in good hands," she whispered. "Best people I could have taking care of me." She looked through them again.

Ben walked to the far corner of the platform. He closed the compass, ran his thumbs over its cover, then squeezed it so tight he felt the plastic cutting into his palm. She trusted him. He had failed. He squatted at the edge of the chickee, shivering in the sun, arms tight across his ribs to ease the ache trying to rip them apart.

## 2

*The way Petey Martinelli tells it at the VFW, the Gates kid did good – ducked and ran, ignored the ordnance going off and the orders to stop. Covered 50 feet of dried mud between the river and that piece of crap barge just like that.*

*Petey was in the Sheriff's special auxiliary at the time – volunteered to keep from rotting away like the rest of us who retired down here for the cheap living. Only 'cheap' ain't always 'good.' He ended up like the rest of us – swapping war stories and sucking down Gennee Creams at 10:00 a.m. – but he fought it for a while.*

*Anyway, Petey says that night four, maybe five kinds of law enforcement come crashing through the brush from all directions, guns drawn and lights bouncing, all hot after the kid. Some in SWAT gear, some camoed, some in plain brown, and all yelling – "Sheriff's Office!" "Federal Agents!" "FDLE!" – he couldn't keep track of it all.*

*The first wave hit Henry Moton's trip wires before the kid was halfway to the barge, and all hell busted loose. Flares, smoke, rockets – whatever homemade crap that crazy Moton kid could rig – BOOM! BAM! All around the perimeter.*

*The Gates kid, though, he stayed on-mission. And Martinelli'd know. Said that kid scaled the hull, rolled across the deck, under the canvas awning and dropped into the hold.*

*"Woulda put my boys at Abu Seif to shame," Petey would say to any who would listen.*

*The Gates kid was headed back out with the Barnes girl when SWAT tossed in the flash-bang. The kid told Petey later it was like someone slammed him against the metal wall, deaf and half blind from the blast – not that he could have seen anything in there through the smoke pouring out that canister.*

*Now, that kid knew squat about the asshat Mangrove Underground. Had no idea where Henry Moton was. Or that his crook of a father was in there, too. All he cared about was his girl. Slung her across his shoulders and climbed like a trooper. After everything he'd been through that day, hauling her up had to have been a chore, even with her a slip of a thing.*

*Anyway, next Martinelli seen of the Gates kid was his head poking through the hatch, then Kelly Barnes limp over his shoulders. Said the kid blinked a couple of times at all the weapons leveled at him, then kind of squinted, deaf to them yelling to show his hands.*

*"We'd passed them both down to officers on the ground," Petey liked to say, "and were starting back for the river when, BA-WHOOM! That barge went up like an ammo dump!" Said flames shot up twenty feet, through the awnings and into the cypress limbs. The Gates kid got across*

21

*the clearing and knelt down, girl in his arms, like nothing else existed.*

*"Could have been a bronze statue in a park," Martinelli would say. Hell, they all stood there, nothing to do but watch the barge burn. They was all way back, not sure what kind of ordnance that crazy Moton punk had stashed. The girl watched, too, big-eyed, like it was the end of the world.*

*She coughed then, shaking her and Gates both. He wiped her hair from her face, kissed her forehead. "You're all right," he said, too loud. "You're safe."*

*She jumped, stared wild-eyed from the fire, to Petey and the deputies, and back to the Gates kid.*

*"Your dad!" she yelled. "Your dad's still in there!"*

*Martinelli said the way the kid stared at her, he didn't have enough hearing back to know what she was saying. He was ashamed of his dad – who wouldn't be? But not enough to let him die like that. Anybody says otherwise is out of line – and Petey'll take a piece out of anyone dares say different. He says the kid stood and turned toward the barge, following where the girl was pointing more than anything.*

*Some of the deputies turned, too, surprised. They all knew Moton had snatched the Barnes girl. But no one guessed he was crazy enough to snatch a county commissioner, too. Probably should have, given it was a Moton and a Gates.*

*So the flames kicked higher and the cypress limbs burned. Martinelli, he swears something clicked with the Gates kid then, some kind of understanding, because he slowly stepped toward the barge.*

Petey grabbed at him. Gates pulled away, stepped again and half-ran, Petey right behind him, until they could feel the heat coming off that steel hull. Gates'd have climbed in if Petey hadn't tackled him, pulled him back.

Through all of this the Barnes girl was screaming, "He'll die! He'll die!" That's where some of the rumors started. But they held Gates back, Petey and the others, no matter what anyone says. No way anyone could have gone in there and lived. The kid knew it, too, because Petey said he didn't fight too much.

That's when the guy in camo broke from the trees and climbed the hull faster than the Gates kid had. A minute, a second later he climbed out again, black against the flames, rag across his nose and mouth and James Gates, still in a coat-and-tie, draped over him.

"Bravest thing I ever seen," Petey said, "no matter who it was." They ran to grab James Gates without paying much attention to the other guy. The rescuer, he dropped and shoved a strongbox into Ben Gates' gut – the same strongbox that caused so much trouble later.

"Do us right, compadre," he said and bolted before anyone could react, Petey would say. Don't know that anyone besides Martinelli and the kid heard him, and I'm not too sure about the kid. Then, POOF! the guy's gone.

Now, later on come the conspiracy theories, the internal investigations, the accusations of who let the Moton kid get away.

Sam Archer, from Parks, sorted things out, put to rest all the B.S. about Henry Moton having a gang of helpers,

23

*about fake FBI agents in the bushes, about cover-ups and politics and payoffs. The only actual facts, he told everyone, were that Henry Moton was the only bad guy out there that night, that he was gone, and that the documents that put James Gates and his buddies away were recovered by a Park Service employee – Gates' son.*

*"The Park Service gave its all for this community," Archer told the media weasels the next day. "You'll have to ask the sheriff's office why it took 20 men to lose Mr. Moton." That stung, but he was right. We screwed that pooch, but that's off the point.*

*Thing is, on the boat ride back, Martinelli said neither Ben nor Kelly looked at one another, boyfriend/girlfriend or no. Or talked any. Like Kelly blamed him for not saving his dad. Like Ben blamed himself. Lost a lot of respect for her that night, Petey said. And gained a lot for the Gates kid. Nut-case Moton had saved James Gates, but Ben would have beat him to it if Petey hadn't held him back. Petey blamed himself for that for a long while. Ben Gates was a good kid. And like Martinelli would say, it took guts the way he saved the Barnes girl. Guts to turn in his own father, you know?*

*No, Ben Gates, he did all right. Petey told him so. We all did. But he wouldn't hear it. You could tell. Spent the rest of his life hiding from that. Trying to make up for that's what got him in so much trouble later.*

*But the kid did better than most would've. That's what Petey Martinelli says, and he would know.*

*Now, locals'll tell you Henry Moton's still out there.*

*Campers talk about food and water disappearing, campfires getting pissed on, boats being cut loose at night. Hunters talk about things shadowing them through the mangroves, or of waking to see a shaggy figure rummaging through their gear.*

*Of course, there's never any proof – just stories. Hell, even in town, anything goes missing, Henry Moton gets the blame. They swear he's out there, watching, waiting. And people still fly that jackoff 'Mangrove Underground' flag, like it ever stood for anything besides a Section Eight washout getting drunk and stupid. Swamp people. They think with their hearts, not their brains, you know?*

3
—

The eastern horizon glowed burnt orange with smoke and the coming sun. The Forestry fire crew at the landing pad eyed Ben sidelong in the pre-dawn light, stopping conversation, suspicious why a Parks administrator was gearing up with them. Wondering if he was qualified. Kelly had laughed when Ben asked to ride along, verify first-hand her reports of mysterious spot fires keeping the main fire going.

"Uh uh, dude. Think you're a tourist, out for a stroll? You're trained. As best I could, anyway. We'll get an honest day's work out of you."

At the pad, only Bailey Jenkins nodded a greeting, but he and Ben had trained together, grown up together.

"Sorry about your place, Bailey," Ben said. "Your mama doing OK?"

"Well as can be expected." Bailey shrugged. Shadows under his bloodshot eyes. Two day stubble. Pushing himself too hard.

"I'm here to keep an eye on you for her." Ben smiled, slapped Bailey on the back. They had had their differences, but the fires had brought the community together.

The Bell 205 slewed in the tailwind flying out. Ben ran his thumb over the outline of the battered Silva compass in his shirt pocket, felt himself relax despite being wedged between Forestry firefighters. He was doing something, taking action.

A brown haze rose in front of them, brightening to rust, then red where the rising sun burned through it. The helicopters slowed, circled a line of wooded hummocks. The Mounds, broad heaps of clay and discarded shells left by the native Calusa five centuries before, now overgrown with oaks and palms.

The Mounds ran northeast-southwest, the easternmost outlier of a series of similar ridges to the west, toward Cypress City. Mud and cord grass expanses surrounded them, making the oaks the only concentrated fuel source in the area. If the crew could stop the fire here, keep it from leap-frogging to the hummocks to the west, the flames would burn themselves out for good.

The crew rappelled to the hummock. The helicopters banked away, and the air was filled with clanking as the crew divided fire rakes, pulaski fire axes, and drip torches among them. Kelly ordered a separate cache of supplies – water, food, oxygen bottles – stacked in the clearing. This was their fallback position and pickup point if the fire cut them off. Their secondary escape route was north, through two miles of marsh, to an abandoned railroad dike.

Kelly formed the crew in a staggered line along the hummock's eastern edge. The approaching smoke hung dark above the distant palms.

Ben took his place in the line beside Bailey, bent double with his pulaski and began clearing brush, dried leaves, and roots along the mound's base. He dug and scraped in time with Bailey, matching him step-for-step, ignoring time and the amount of ground he had cleared. They had reached the end of the first hummock when Ben smelled smoke.

"Come on, Grandpa." Bailey, wild-eyed, daring Ben to keep up. Ben followed, slogging through the serrated cord grass to the next hummock. Behind him, boots of others squished in the mud, seemingly on Ben's heels. Once across, they all hunched over again, extending the fire line along this hummock's base.

Ben straightened, back crackling. Upwind, the wall of smoke towered above the chest-high cord grass, closer now, though he could see no flames. The pulaski – part axe, part mattock – dragged heavy. His hands ached despite his thick gloves. The asbestos fire suit tugged at him, made every movement take twice as long as it should.

The man next to him, Palmer, tapped Ben on the ankle with his pulaski. Ben smarted from more than the tap. The other man had caught up with him, reminded Ben he wasn't working as quickly as others on the line. Palmer, hired a month ago, working with the Park's number two man for the first time. On the line, respect was earned.

Ben bent back to work, falling into the once-ingrained rhythm of dig-and-scrape. "Asses and elbows!" Kelly had yelled a decade earlier during Forestry training, until he and the other trainees heard it in their sleep. "I better not see anything but asses and elbows!"

Smoke thickened as they neared the end of the mound. Firefighters along the line wet bandanas and tied them across their noses and mouths, pulled on their goggles. Ben stared, stunned for a moment to see some firefighters tying kerchief-sized Mangrove Underground flags sold in Cypress City gift shops across their faces. Smoke boiled up 100 yards across the grass flats. The crew quickened its pace. Ben's pulaski grew heavier. He glanced at his watch. Ten o'clock. By now Sam Archer, the Park superintendent, had to know he was gone.

"Asses and elbows," Ben chanted to himself with each stroke, letting the rhythm carry him. "Asses and elbows."

Smoke curled around them. Flames crackled in the dry grass. Ben scraped quicker, trusting his long-ago training. The ache in his back and hands disappeared. Slowly, he gained on Bailey. After this hummock, they had only one more to go. He'd show them an office-jockey could still work a fire line.

The wind gusted then, and the heat hit him. Fire roared across the grass flats, a wall of flame 12 feet high. Sparks drifted into the tinder-dry grass, spreading small spot fires ahead of the main fire. Now was the critical stage – if they could stop the flames from crossing their fire line, the fire would burn itself out. If not, it would burn through the hummocks and the grass behind faster than any of them could run.

Out of habit, Ben checked the position of the firefighters around him, making sure there were no gaps where the flames could break through. He needn't have worried. Kelly had trained them well. The crew had tightened their ranks, digging at twice their former speed. Pulaskis were replaced with shovels and fire rakes as yellow-clad figures scurried behind the fire trench, ready to put out any stray sparks that crossed onto the mound.

Heat eddied, clearing the air. Fire whirls rose in the grass, miniature tornadoes spawned by the fire's convective heat and the gusting wind. Ben looked to tree tops behind him. Whirls could lift sparks hundreds of feet off the ground, into the trees' crowns where the crew would have no chance to stop them. If the flames caught there, the resulting fire could draw up all the oxygen from ground level, supercharging the fire. The crew's only option then would be to run like hell. Only, they couldn't run in mud.

The oaks wavered in the haze, but showed no signs of flame. On the ground, though, six feet behind the fire trench, stray sparks had ignited dry leaves. Ben leapt to put them out, yelling to one of the shovelers to help.

There was shouting then. North, on the small mound they had yet to reach, the trees burst into flame, sending a column of fire roaring upward. Ben and the others rushed to the end of their hummock, quickly scraping a makeshift trench to keep the fire from spreading south, back down the hummock line. Kelly yelled into a two-way radio, demanding water drops from any aircraft available.

Ben scanned the surrounding underbrush as he dug, alert for stray sparks. Kelly was beside him then, yelling for the crew to dig back along the mound's western flank, shouting for them to widen the trench. She eyed the trees towering behind them, too. This mound was larger, more densely wooded than the other. If the flames jumped across and ignited in the hardwoods here, their escape route back down the hummocks could be cut off.

By now sparks had caught in the dry grass to the west, surrounding the crew on three sides. Kelly pressed a shovel to Ben's chest, then ran to the far end of the line. Ben joined other firefighters squashing sparks in the dry leaves.

The others around him, the newbies, moved tense and jerky, unlike their smooth digging earlier. Smoke blew thicker. Ben coughed, choked, heard others doing the same. Flames from the northern hummock advanced toward them across the narrow flats. Ben shouted a warning. The crew responded to him as quickly as they had to Kelly, rushing to widen the swath of cleared ground between them and the flames. Hot wind seared his exposed cheeks.

A shout behind him, then a roar that seemed to come from everywhere. Embers rained from the high branches. The fire had leaped their just-dug line and caught in the crowns of the oaks behind. The air cleared. An oppressive heat rolled over him, though the leaves on the ground were not burning.

"Run!" Ben pointed back toward their landing zone, down the hummock's unforested lower slope. He needn't have bothered. The firefighters were already sprinting. Fire in the tree crowns, and the hot, clear air meant the oak grove was about to burst into flame from tree top to the ground. A few seconds' hesitation could be the difference in escaping or dying.

Ben turned, shouting to a straggler, thought he heard a higher-pitched echo of his voice, realized Kelly was yelling as well, sending others in the crew running ahead of her. Branches fell, flying sideways, igniting as they flew. Ben ran, pacing Kelly.

He glanced over his shoulder. A lone firefighter wavered behind by the grass flats. Ben stopped, cursing. The man dropped his shovel and fell to his knees. Ben ran back, grabbed the man, and tried to help him stand. The man coughed, gagged, shaking in Ben's grip. Ben grabbed him with both hands, pulled him uphill, away from the burning grass. The man barely moved. Desperate, Ben knelt, ducked his head under the man's torso and swung him up onto his shoulders. He stood, legs nearly buckling with the effort, and started back toward the pickup point.

Flames covered the mound, snaking down the tree trunks, erupting outward. At the hummock's base, a figure beckoned. Kelly, at the last remaining gap in the fire, shouting something Ben couldn't hear. Ben took a step toward her and knew he would never reach the gap in time. Behind him, the grass fire had reached the fire trench, the flames taller than his head. For an instant he imagined it was Kelly he carried. His father's face, and Henry Moton's, loomed in his mind. Would he die like Henry, then?

A voice from training echoed in his head, pushed all other thoughts aside. "Choose where the fire hits you!" He'd hammered the same last-ditch survival adage into scores of new recruits. A grass fire burned quicker, but less intense, especially in wet terrain like this. He had a better chance to survive there than in a fully-engulfed hardwood grove. If the wall of flame across the grass was thin, and he was lucky, he could carry the man through it and into the relative safety of the burned grass flats beyond. Ben staggered downslope, building momentum, took a deep breath and plunged into the flames.

The heat tore at him, even through his asbestos suit. The marshy soil clutched at his feet, nearly tripping him. Ben stumbled on in a slow-motion sprint with all the energy he could muster. Five steps more, a sixth. His legs gave way and he sunk knee-first in the hot mud. Hot. But not burning. Ben opened his eyes. He was through. Cord grass clumps smoldered around him. His face stung. But he was alive. The man across his shoulders hung unmoving. Ben's lungs ached, his body shook, but he couldn't rest here. He lurched to his feet.

Behind him, the larger hummock was solid flames. Ahead, only smoke rose from the smaller mound where the spot fire had started. The fire had rolled over it so fast, and the mound was so small, the flames hadn't fully taken hold.

Ben slogged the thirty yards to solid ground and dropped to his knees again.

Smoke twisted up from the scorched earth, like steam on the Gulf in winter. Ashes fell white around him, as if he were caught in a snow storm. Ben slid the unconscious man onto the still-warm ground. He pulled off his own gloves, his goggles, his bandana, and checked himself for burns. He seemed unscathed. He peeled off the other man's goggles and bandana. Bailey Jenkins. Breathing, if barely, pulse throbbing faint at his throat.

The world blurred. Ben was aware of talking to Bailey, of sitting him upright, of holding him as Bailey coughed so hard Ben's ribs shook. Kelly and the other firefighters were beyond the flames. If they had survived. Bailey was all Ben knew, all he had left. They had failed, all of them. The fire was still roaring toward Cypress City, and he had no way to warn the town.

Helicopter rotors pulsed overhead. That was right. The National Guard would see the fire, radio a warning. They would see him and Bailey, maybe, send help, and lift them to safety. He held Bailey, whispered to him about the helicopters, nodded to Bailey's mumbled replies. The helicopter sound spun around him. Or the hummock spun. Ben imagined he heard water cascading, flames hissing and sputtering somewhere far away.

Shadow-figures appeared from the smoke. Firefighters. A fresh crew sent out to help? Men knelt beside him, pulled him and Bailey farther upslope, leaned them against a

34

scorched palm trunk. A green oxygen cylinder appeared, connected by thin tubing to a clear facemask. Hands pressed the mask over Bailey's nose and mouth.

"Others! There!" Ben pointed back down the hummock line. They had to find Kelly and the crew.

More aircraft sounded overhead, the deeper pitch of twin turboprops. A Forestry air tanker rained a long line of pink-tinged fire retardant across the swamp, blocking the fire's advance.

"You're stupid-crazy. You know that?" Kelly glared down at him. Ben blinked to make sure he wasn't imagining her. She knelt beside him. "And absolutely incredible." She looked to the men helping Bailey. "How's he doing?"

The men helping Bailey shrugged, noncommittal.

"The fire...?" Ben said, surprised by the rough sound of his voice.

"Turned, except for the mop-up." She smiled at Ben's puzzled expression. "It blew up on us, but water drops took care of the hummocks and tankers sealed it off to the west. Fresh crews helped, too." She nodded at the new men with Bailey.

The rest of Kelly's crew was there then, cheering when they saw Ben and Bailey. Several slapped Ben on the back, nodded their approval.

"Everyone...?"

"All good. *They* had the sense to run *away* from the fire. No, no. You rocked, Ben. We regrouped, waited for the water drops, then came to find you."

Bailey coughed, tried to hold the oxygen mask himself, then shook with another series of racking spasms.

"He needs outta here. ASAP. Sosa! Med-evac!" A man behind them bent over a two-way radio. "Idiot!" Kelly put a hand on Bailey's forehead. "Playing hero. I shouldn't have kept him on the line."

Ben shook his head. "He needed to be here. He just ... hung back."

"You and fiery rescues." Kelly smiled so quickly Ben could have imagined it. "He owes you a steak dinner." Ben glanced past Bailey, taking in the full scene for the first time. The mound still smoldered around them, blackened. The next hummock over, where Ben and Bailey had almost been trapped, smoldered as well, free of flame.

"We saved these, too." She tossed him a small canvas knapsack. An apple and some Granola bars fell out. She handed him a canteen. "You sure you're OK?"

Ben nodded, sipped at the water. The fire was turned, though the airplanes and helicopters had more to do with that than the crew's fire trenches. And he had saved Bailey.

Kelly picked up the apple, bit into it, and followed his gaze. "New crews get the mop-up." She looked to Bailey again. "We're out of here. Debrief, figure what happened. This was *way* too close."

"Your mystery spot fires?"

"Give them 15 minutes. Back that way." Kelly pointed west, toward Cypress City.

Ben glanced at his watch. Not quite 2 p.m. Had he been out here so long? Sam Archer would be fuming. Bailey coughed then, and thoughts of Sam evaporated. Bailey, alive, justified skipping all the press conferences in the world, even if it cost Ben his job.

"We'll see," Ben said. The afternoon winds were already shifting westward. There was no way embers from these hummocks could spread any farther that direction. "It breaks out back there, I owe you a steak dinner. Ben settled back on his haunches, sipping water, and watched the fresh crews rooting out hidden hot spots on the hummock, some men feeling the ground with their bare hands to make certain there were no embers left burning to re-ignite.

Overhead, a formation of National Guard Blackhawks sped west, sweeping the area behind them for any flare-ups.

## 4

"*SafariLand's hard to explain now a-days,*" said DeWayne Wilson, who ran the attraction before it went under. "*The new cineplex is there now, but back in the boom-days that park was the only reason tourists pulled off 441 and left their money here.*

"*The mermaids were the draw, of course. And that dark, air-conditioned amphitheater was a welcome break from the heat. 'Cool, azure waters beckoning,' the billboards used to read. 'An underwater paradise filled with adventure for young and old alike!' Plate glass panels stretched 100 feet wide and 30 feet high across one wall, and beyond that was the spring.*

"*You can see it, can't you – water weeds swaying around the rock ledge of the stage, bubbles from the hidden air hoses streaming up, like water monsters are hiding just out of sight? And all the while, inside the theater, springlight flickering blue and green, mesmerizing, across 500 velour seats climbing up the back of the cavern, across 500 eager faces. It was a class act, and a far cry from today's circus-ride parks.*

"Now, Ben Gates always had a flair for the sensational – quick to gild everything he said, everything he did. Just like his daddy. No great loss Delmore Moton finally finished off that clan.

"I'd seen Ben and Kelly Barnes grow up – like they were my own kids. Ben was trouble, but Kelly was all sweetheart.

"I remember the day. Explicitly. It was right before Henry dragged Kelly off, and Ben did no saving. Or even helping. No, he came back just in time to see Kelly get herself fired – though she expected neither Ben nor the firing. It killed me to lose her.

"I was in the control room, watching guests tramp past, when Ben stumbled in fresh back from the university. He felt his way along the varnished handrail behind the uppermost seats, waiting for his eyes to adjust to the dim light. He stopped, watched a school of mullet swim through the bubbles, circle once, then bank up and out of view.

"An older couple bumped him, and he would have gone ass-over-appetite down the steps if he hadn't caught the nearest seat back and slid into the back row. Guests streamed in past him, down the steps, filling the theater, and I gave him no more thought just then.

"The crowd was rowdy that day, so I tapped the tickle switch, sent a little jolt through Rap-Tor's collar.

"You remember how it was, Rap-Tor thrashing past the glass, legs tucked close and tail flailing? He was 14-feet long, but through that thick glass he looked twice that.

39

*A brown-and-yellow smear of teeth and scales stretching across that theater.*

"*As ever, kids ran down to the windows, pressed their faces close for a better look, their breath fogging the glass. Ben stood, too, like he wanted to join them. He'd finished his exams early and driven in that morning. Left his car outside, still crammed with dirty laundry, and rushed in to see Kelly.*

"*Before he could, though, I slid the curtains closed and dimmed the house lights. The kids scooted back to their seats. I phased in 'Scheherazade' low and started the narration.*

"'Come with me now, back to Hermosa Fountain's darkest pre-history, for Red Riding Hood in 50 Million B.C.' *(I remember the show because Kelly was still wearing her red gingham hood afterwards, swearing she'd done no harm, dripping on my office linoleum all the while.) Overdone, but the tourists loved it. I slid the curtains back open, and they all 'ooohed' and 'aaahed' as the mermaids swam past, smiling and waving and blowing bubbles as they went.*

"*I hit the tickle switch again and Rap-Tor lashed past, ragged-toothed, scattering the girls. If you knew just where to look you could make out a hint of the Plexiglas panel dividing the spring. Rap-Tor swam closest to the audience, while the mermaids performed safe on the far side.*

"At 'Red Riding Hood came walking through the forest,' *Kelly made her entrance, sequined tail flashing and black hair streaming. Ben leaned forward, back straight.*

"*She had that effect. The other girls swam beautifully, professional athletes. But Kelly flowed, like the tail was*

40

*part of her. That day she slowed, smiled, and waved as she reached center stage. Most people waved back. Except Ben. You can just see him, can't you, sitting there like stone, mouth open.*

"*The other mermaids ducked offstage for air then, but Kelly stayed, swimming for minutes, hours it seemed, without a breath. And all the while acting out Red's story as I told it. (I was piped in through underwater speakers, you remember.)*

"*When I said,* 'Red ran from the wolf,' *Kelly looped past Rap-Tor, hands to her mouth, face full of terror.*

"*When I said,* 'Red knelt by Grandma's bed,' *she settled next to the old croc. And never a breath in between. It wasn't natural.*

"*Through all this, Ben didn't move. I knew how he felt. In that spring Kelly was alive in ways you could have only guessed at before, though you'd known her all her life. When the other mermaids were offstage, she would hover in front of you, like only you and she existed, the two of you floating alone in some other fairytale place-and-time.*

"*I say I know how Ben felt because just then I saw him reach toward Kelly where she hung like a doll in the blue. For a moment it looked like he could take her, pluck her from that two-dimensional scene.*

"*Then his hand passed through her, or past her, and kept going, black and empty against the bright spring. The crowd murmured, sensing something special was happening. I forced myself back to the narration. Kelly was that captivating.*

"How can I describe it now? This is what makes everything stand out so clearly: through all this, Kelly circled Rap-Tor, crossed over him and around him like I'd never seen her do, holding her arms out as if asking him to dance.

"Sunlight winked off the Plexiglas divider. Kelly swam past again. The glare disappeared for a second. I paused, knowing something was wrong, but not sure exactly what.

"Two, maybe three seconds went by before it registered: Kelly had blocked the glare. She was in Rap-Tor's side of the spring.

"Ben noticed it, too, because he jumped up, like he'd run to help her. But he was glued to the spot, scared as me that if he took his eyes from her it would break the spell, make Rap-Tor turn on her. I don't know how else to explain it – like nothing bad had happened yet, and that if I didn't move – or even breathe – nothing would keep on happening.

"Part of me realized Kelly was the only girl still in the water, but all I could do was watch.

"She motioned with one hand and Rap-Tor swam up and past the windows. Kelly looped around him in big spirals, patting his head as she went past. Every word of this is true, now. You can look it up in the archives.

"Ben reached out again, in slow-motion, as if to pull her through the glass. The cavern was silent. Then I realized I didn't know how long it had been since I had stopped talking.

"Of course, that croc could have gone for Kelly any second – he'd done it to handlers before, you recall. Kelly seemed in control, though. Her best chance lay in letting her be.

"Now, Ben and Kelly had grown up best friends – don't ask me why, but I'd seen it myself. They'd dated through most of high school and had kept in touch while Ben was off at school. But there in that theater I think Ben for *the first time saw how far beyond him she was – how she was tuned into something he'd never know, no matter how he tried in all the years after.*

"Beth Gates, his mama, had been like that, too, and I think at that moment Ben realized he'd never have understood her either, any more than he understood Kelly.

"He was too selfish – he never could give up enough of himself to be part of someone or something bigger. As it was, he stood there, bone-still, scared for Kelly, sure, but also scared of Kelly.

"After what seemed forever, Rap-Tor settled to center stage. Kelly did a slow figure-eight over him, then kicked offstage like there was no hurry or concern. People in the theater were whispering then, but only vaguely aware of what had just happened.

"Ben looked around, like he just then realized other people were there. That it had all been real. Then he leaped over the seatback and ran for the dressing room as quick as he could. Guests started streaming out then, and it was a few minutes before I could get through them and to the dressing room myself.

*"Ben had already forced his way in and was hugging Kelly like it was the end of the world, yelling she was crazy, yelling not to scare him like that again – and her still dripping wet and wearing her tail.*

*"The other girls huddled to the side, giving them room. Or giving Kelly room. No one had ever seen anything like that – a girl in a mermaid costume playing with a 14-foot Nile crocodile. She should have been dead, and we all knew it.*

*"I don't think Kelly did, though. She looked in another world. Happy, but dazed. And perplexed, as if she didn't understand what all the fuss was about. She said as much later. At length. I had to threaten Ben with the police to pry him free of Kelly and get her into my office.*

*"I had to fire her, of course. That hurt. But there was no avoiding it. The phones were already ringing with lawyers and insurance adjusters and chamber of commerce members and Judge Barnes himself before it was all over.*

*"I tried to hire her back next afternoon, but the damage had been done. Two days later she helped Henry Moton and Bailey Jenkins crash the show, and you know how that turned out. Henry's brain-child, the Mangrove Underground, was as juvenile as it was short-lived. But it by-God grabbed folks' attention. Still does. A grand act of defiance against inevitable change.*

*Anyway, Kelly went straight to firefighter school after that. A waste of talent, but that takes nothing away from what she did that day. She'll always be magic, a heartbreaker in the best sense of the word."*

## 5

Ben was still sipping water when a succession of black clouds mushroomed into the too-blue western horizon, where the National Guard helicopters had disappeared minutes before. Miles behind the hummock line where Ben and the fire crew rested. Ben leaned back against a scorched palm tree and closed his eyes to shut out the sight. His eyes burned. His throat ached from the brown haze still rising off the charred cord grass surrounding the mud island. Kelly was right.

Around him the crew sat in small groups, leaning back-to-back or against blackened palm trunks, water bottles out, heads down. Beside him two firefighters had peeled the bulky yellow asbestos jacket from a limp Bailey Jenkins and were pouring water over Bailey's head. He was breathing but was unconscious again. This wasn't right.

Ben forced his emotions aside and focused on the rising smoke. He hadn't believed Kelly's reports. Not really. They hadn't made sense. But squatting here in the mud with the Forestry crew, watching the black billow up... Maybe the Guard had seen someone this time. The fires must have ignited right beneath them.

"Could be one of us," Sam Archer had said the day before. Ben glanced at the crew. A firefighter was the obvious guess. But who? One of a dozen of these kids with Mangrove Underground bandannas hanging loose around their necks? No. Unless he or she had an accomplice who could spark a fire from five miles away. With that logic, it could be any of the locals in town who had taken to flying Mangrove Underground flags lately.

Two men with flag bandannas huddled by Bailey Jenkins. Why had Bailey hung back? Bailey knew how to cover up arson, had been hip-deep in Henry Moton's craziness... but so had Kelly. And Ben himself. No. That was lifetimes ago. Bailey had been pushing himself hard since his folks' house had burned, taking stupid risks. He wouldn't have burned his family's homestead.

A breeze brushed Ben's cheek, a hint of the afternoon easterlies. The rising wind would fan the new fires, and drive them closer to Cypress City.

"Same song, fourth verse!" Kelly flung her half-eaten apple across the ash-scummed marsh. It disappeared in the smoke before Ben heard the splash. The reflective 'Chief' on the back of her jacket rippled silvery as she spun. "Just as the wind shifts." Her braided ponytail flew out straight as she turned back to Ben. Her face was a dark collage of smudges except for the pale rings around her eyes where her goggles had been. She glared at Ben and pointed back toward the black smoke plumes. "Tell me that wasn't torched. I dare you."

"I believed you, Kel. I just needed to see it."

"Uh huh." She dropped her voice lower, imitating his. "I believed you, Kel. I just blew it off."

Ben clenched his jaws to keep silent. It wasn't the time or place for this.

Bailey Jenkins coughed and rolled onto his side. Palmer pressed the oxygen mask tighter over his nose and mouth. Bailey lay still, not seeming to notice. Bobby Peddiway swatted at the clots of mosquitoes swarming over Bailey's exposed shoulders. Beyond them, other firefighters were stripping off their heavy jackets, or staring expressionless across the burned cord grass.

"They're exhausted, Ben. We can't keep this up!" Kelly's voice slapped at him. "What does it take to find a torch?" She nodded toward Bailey. "If that wind had shifted 10 minutes earlier..."

Ben took two deep breaths, calming himself. She was right. They could all be laying there like Bailey. He had waited too long to act. He needed to find how the fires were starting. Who was setting them? Whoever it was knew what they were doing, but this crew... no. They were here, risking their lives. No one was that crazy. The idea clung to him, though. He wanted to ask Kelly, but that would have to wait until they were back in town, in private.

"This one we just beat, it started the same way yesterday?" He spoke low so only Kelly could hear.

Kelly looked down and ground Granola crumbs into the hard-pack mud with the toe of her boot. She glanced back up at Ben, thin-lipped. "Like my reports said, we drop back twenty miles or so, wherever there's enough solid ground to maneuver, we cut a line, let the fire burn itself out. Then we sit in the mud, watch new fires break out behind us and do it all over again. For the last *four* days. It's *not* the same fire, Ben. But it has to be the same person."

Ben nodded. "I had to be sure. We're so short-handed. Sam's gonna ream me when I get back."

"You want a medal?" Kelly's voice was louder. Around them, men and women in scorched yellow fire gear turned to listen.

"No. Answers." Ben kept his voice low, his tone even. "National Guard spotters say they're spontaneous. Official word is still 'lightning igniting cane field runoff.'"

"Burning fertilizer? Ben, you know better! Nothing out here burns that black. Not on its own anyway!" A few firefighters edged closer, straining to hear what Ben said. "Sorry," Kelly said. "Bailey's got me... if this fire hadn't 'restarted,' he wouldn't be hurt."

"I think Henry Moton's back." Bobby Peddiway looked up from Bailey Jenkins.

"Weird stuff happens on these Indian mounds," said someone else. Others murmured, nodded.

"It is not Henry Moton!" Ben turned to the group, his voice louder than he meant it to be. The stories, like the red-and-black flags, refused to go away. The crew froze, startled by Ben's tone. Bobby Peddiway looked away. "It's not swamp spirits," Ben said quieter, "or skunk apes or space aliens. We're here to put out fires, not chase boogie men."

"Henry's not the boogie man," Kelly said.

"Was." A new suspicion sprung full-formed in Ben's head at 'Henry's not.' "And gone for years. Right?" Ben watched Kelly's eyes. She had been more involved with the Mangrove Underground, with Henry, than Bailey. Was she a firebug, carrying on Henry's legacy? There was no sound from the firefighters around them. Even sounds of the wind and crackling cord grass died away.

Kelly glared. "You'd know better than I would."

Ben looked away. He had stopped Henry but lost two friends and his own father in the process. They had put this to rest long ago, he and Kelly. But one offhand remark from Sam Archer made it seem as fresh as yesterday. Kelly's, too, it seemed. "This has nothing to do with ghosts," he finally said, his voice cracking as he tried to speak low and steady. Kelly looked away, too. "Sorry."

Ben stared across the burned wetlands, re-collecting his thoughts. Obsessing on the past, pointing fingers wouldn't help this crew, the Park, or the town. The situation was complicated enough.

To the west, a brown haze was spreading, a dirty smudge below the black smoke. "Burning lighter as the grass catches," Ben said to himself. "Phosphates and mercury, it'd burn black until it hit the Gulf."

"Yeah." Kelly's voice was a whisper beside him. "We gonna find who's doing it?"

"I need *proof* before I talk to Sam again. You heard him yesterday. He doesn't want to hear it." Ben spoke softly so the others wouldn't overhear. "Last night ABC called this the biggest screw-up since the Yellowstone fires. The *Times* is talking drug-field feuds and neo-Batista militia. It's getting crazy back there."

"It's been crazy out here. You playing politics while we risk our lives doesn't help." Kelly looked back at Bailey's unconscious form. "These are your people, Ben." Her voice grew louder. "We gonna stop this now, or will we lose someone?"

Ben grabbed her arm and pulled her away from the group. His face burned, as if the hummock had re-ignited. He wasn't sure if it was his hand or her arm that was shaking. Above them, so mewhere, the rotors of a Forest Service 205 pulsed deeper, louder, coming to take the crew to safety. "Kelly, I've probably lost my job being here. But I'm here." Ben forced his teeth to unclench. "You have a problem, talk to me, not the whole damn world!"

Kelly pulled free. "Your job? This is life-and-death." She pointed at Bailey. "You should know that better than anyone. Some pencil-pusher drops my crew into an out of control fire for no reason, it's everyone's problem. They'll damn-sure be part of this discussion!"

"Hey! I'm on it!"

"What does that mean, Ben?"

"Shut up *one* minute you'd..." Ben glanced at the blackening horizon then exhaled slow.

"I'm tired of the talking, Ben. Bottom line, someone's out here..."

"Bottom line, Kel, there's 50,000 acres gone, houses have burned, Bailey needs the hospital, and fires are still burning toward town. You put out the fires. *I'll* find who's setting them."

"When?"

"Get me a chopper. You fly back to town, I'll go hunting. Deal?"

Kelly started to speak, then glanced at her crew. She spoke quietly again, as if to herself. "We can't do this much longer. Physically or mentally. It's like, the only reason we're out here is to make the CNN news loop." She turned to Ben, eyes narrowed. "You promise you're going after him? No planning a strategy, no 'I'll check with Sam.' You? Personally? Now?"

Ben nodded. He would find out all he could before he flew back to town. What could Sam do, fire him twice? Kelly was still watching him.

"Follow through, Ben. Please."

Ben studied her, unable to speak, unable even to form the right words in his mind. Kelly held his gaze for several seconds, then turned away. "Sosa! Get a ride for office boy. He's going hunting."

The crew stood, stretched, shrugged back into their heavy asbestos jackets, slung packs back over their shoulders, and collected scorched drip torches and other bits of scattered gear.

"Dust-off's on its way, Kelly!" Nestor Sosa yelled. "No spares, though. Ben mind riding with the Guard?"

51

"Even better!" Ben yelled back. He looked at Kelly. "I need to talk to some Guard pilots, anyway. To follow through."

Kelly rolled her eyes. "Let's go, folks. Hot food and showers going to waste." She stepped away without looking to see if the others were following, her shoulders and hips flowing as if she were swimming through the mud and standing water. Four men lifted Bailey on a makeshift stretcher of shovel handles and fire jackets. Another lay the oxygen bottle on the stretcher and held the mask to Bailey's face.

Ben fell in at the end of the line as they slogged single-file through knee-deep muck toward the raised railroad bed a mile to the north. Within a dozen steps they were back in the untouched cord grass flats behind their burn line. The chest-high grass ripped at his jumpsuit, buzzing like new corduroy. The wind shifted, swirling the brown smoke around them again, as if the swamp had exhaled some dark poison. Ben's eyes watered. The others became ghostly shapes fading in front of him. He wiped his eyes with muddy hands and covered his nose and mouth with a wet bandana. The man two steps ahead, Palmer, was an orange shadow in the brown murk.

It wasn't Henry starting these fires. But a copycat? Setting fires and spreading the Mangrove Underground flags in town? So many new people on the fire crews, kids really, taken with the old stories. Could one of them know some-thing? This was crazy without actual evidence, a dog chasing its tail.

Ben focused on the mud in front of him, on the sludge flowing into the holes from Palmer's boots, erasing any trace of his passing. He touched his chest pocket, ran his fingers over his compass. He couldn't imagine four, five days of this. Ben stopped, pulled his cell phone from his belt, checking for messages. Nothing. Too far from anywhere to get a signal. Ben switched the phone off, saving the battery. He would deal with phone messages soon enough. He looked up. The fire crew was gone.

The smoke around him thickened, coalesced into vague shapes that spun away as quickly as they formed. Palmer's footsteps had disappeared. Ben lunged forward to catch up with the others, as if dream-running in quicksand. He couldn't get lost. Not now. He slogged on, breath rasping. Walking shapes appeared to either side. He slowed and they dispersed back into smoke. Ben glanced at the mud behind him to get his bearings, but his footsteps had already filled. He pulled out his compass, face scratched and battered. He would walk north. But a few degrees off and he could miss the group completely in this murk.

He stood still, listening. Boots squashed, gear clanked somewhere nearby, but Ben couldn't tell in which direction. He lurched forward again, in the direction his feet were pointing. Shapes swirled in the smoke again. Ben hadn't thought of the Nunnehi for years until Bobby Peddiway, someone mentioned Indian mounds. He said a silent 'please' to any swamp spirits that might be listening.

The thrumming of helicopter rotors made him look up. He could see nothing but smoke. A steady 'wump-wump

-wump,' more a vibration than a sound, grew louder, shook the air, the cord grass, the mud around his boots and settled somewhere ahead and to his right. The railroad dike couldn't be far off. Guard 'copter – it was too high-pitched for a 205. Ben moved toward the sound. His legs ached, his lungs burned. The smoke thinned. Ten yards ahead shadowy figures were climbing diagonally up the mud-and-gravel slope of the raised railway. Above them the blunt-nosed outline of a helicopter rested on top of the dike, a giant insect lurking in the brown haze. Bigger, broader than the Forestry 'copters Ben was used to, its rotors spun in a slow blur, each blade nearly distinct.

Ben paused at the foot of the dike to catch his breath, let his heart slow. A yellow-clad figure glided down the slope. Kelly. She let a mini-avalanche of gravel carry her the last few feet to Ben.

"Your chariot awaits!" she yelled above the helicopter's howl.

Ben nodded as nonchalant as he could and stepped around her.

Kelly caught his arm, leaned close. "Hey, I trust you."

"Yeah." It was too much: the fire, the Mangrove Underground memories, Sam's suspicions, Bailey on the stretcher. He needed to get above the smoke, above it all, where he could think. And find the source of these fires.

Kelly held his arm. "Talk later?"

Ben nodded again, not daring to speak, and scrambled up to the Blackhawk. She could keep her pep talks. And her condescension. He'd find the firebug, whether she believed in him or not. And it wouldn't be one of this crew.

## 6

*It was Diane Cowper, holding court after the commission meeting:*

*Not to speak ill, but the Ben Gates they all worship never existed. Not the way they tell it, anyway. But these people need something to believe in. Glorifying criminals like the Gates family and Henry Moton gives them that, I suppose.*

*Make no mistake – Ben Gates was up to his neck in that Mangrove Underground garbage. Maybe not at first, when Sam Archer offered him a job, hoping to raise him above his upbringing. But as soon as that Gates boy ran into Henry Moton, it was over. You know how these people stick together.*

*As my beloved Joseph – may God rest his soul – used to point out, the people down here are simply not as advanced as we are. They're not as intelligent, as well-educated. Laws mean nothing to them.*

*Sam found that out the hard way. After the Gates boy had already taken advantage. And still he kept him at the*

*Park all those years, hoping to rehabilitate him. A heart of gold, Sam Archer. But then he was from up north, as well. Trenton, or close to it.*

*Sam was the best thing to happen to this county, my Joseph notwithstanding. He saved the town from James Gates' scams, expanded the Park and slowed the unchecked development, then saved it from Ben Gates' fires a decade later.*

*For Ben to turn on him, destroy a good man's work and reputation after all Sam had done for him...*

*My Joseph had it straight from Sam Archer himself at the Knights of Columbus hall, not long after the investigations were finished.*

*It was out in East Egypt Sam and Ben first met, a few days before the Mangrove Underground business came to a head, on a camping platform Henry Moton and his cronies had burned.*

*Sam went out there specifically to meet the Gates boy, though he didn't tell Ben that. He knew who Ben was, who Ben's father was, that Ben was fixing the camping chickee off the books. He'd heard Ben was a good kid, despite his father, and wanted to see for himself.*

*In fairness, now, I don't think Ben knew who had burned the chickee. Not at first. He was just back after finishing what passes for college down here, earning some extra money and getting away from his drug-running father and his land grabs. Fixing a deck in the middle of nowhere was perfect for that.*

My Joseph said Ben was ripping up burned boards, nailing down new planks in their place, as Sam rounded the point on the big river and turned up the side-creek toward the chickee.

The DEA had been out there tearing up dope fields, so Ben had to have been a little nervous. Or maybe he thought his family name would protect him.

Sam sped to within a few yards of the platform, then cut the wheel and reversed the engines – showing off, getting Ben's attention. The boat settled a foot from the pilings, just like that. I wish I could have seen Ben's face – locals think they're the only ones can handle a boat.

Ben stepped back, hammer held ready. Sam was impressed. That reaction alone told him Ben had some sense. Not many people make it out that far, and the ones who do usually aren't joy-riding.

Sam was smart enough to be cautious, too. He jumped to the deck and grinned, held out his hand, palm down, making sure Ben's hand was empty. 'Sam Archer,' he said.

Ben just shifted his grip on the hammer.

'Not the friendly Park Service welcome I expected.' Sam kept smiling, always diplomatic. He was someone you could trust, though few of these people ever knew how to take him.

'I'm not the friendly Park Service.' Ben glanced past Sam, into the boat, then back to Sam. By then Sam's arm already was reaching behind him. Ben swung the hammer back, ready to fight.

'Whoa! Wallet!' Sam held up his leather billfold. 'You may not be the Park Service, but I sure as hell am.' He let the wallet fall open to show his Park ID card. Assistant Superintendent, he was at the time.

'Sorry.' Ben lowered the hammer. 'This far back, and that bouncer's handshake...' He dropped the hammer, hand shaking.

Ben Gates had always seen himself working for the Park, let everyone know it. That was one reason Sam was out there. But in that moment, Ben thought he'd blown his best chance of that.

Sam wasn't like that, though. 'No worries,' he said. 'Out here, better safe than sorry, huh?' He kept smiling. 'Gates? Like the county commissioner?'

Of course Sam knew Ben's father was James Gates. He just needed to see Ben's reaction, see how close father and son were.

Ben tensed at that, then nodded. My Joseph said that's when Sam decided to hire Ben. Go out of his way to give a local a dream job he'd otherwise never have a chance at. And if Sam got information about a commissioner-gone-bad in the process, well, so be it.

'Who, do you think?' Sam nodded at the burned boards.

'Kids.' Ben shrugged. 'Good time got out of hand.'

'Not pissed-off dopers?' Sam, just like that, letting it hang.

*Ben didn't flinch. 'Growers'd burn your house. Locals with a grudge... People get lost out here all the time.'*

*'So I've heard,' Sam said. 'And I agree. About the kids. Good reasoning.' Sam was like that. Always building people up.*

*Sam stepped into his boat and pulled two beers and a Subway sandwich from a cooler. He handed a beer to Ben and sat down on the new decking, laying the sandwich between them. 'You like roast beef? No way I can eat the whole thing.' Like I said, a good guy.*

*Ben sat beside him, watching Sam from the corner of his eye. Sam sipped his beer, looked close at the work Ben had been doing. Finally, Ben picked up the half-sandwich. They ate slowly, neither talking until the food was gone and their beers empty. The wind was picking up and the big river glittering with the rising chop. Clouds were building, and they knew the afternoon thunderstorms weren't far off.*

*'Shame the way all these developments are pinching in on this place, don't you think?' Sam finally said, sounding Ben out.*

*Ben stared into his beer bottle, like he didn't know how to answer. 'We used to camp out here when I was little, me and my folks,' he said. 'We'd catch dinner every night. No more. Mercury, e. coli, no telling what you'd be eating."*

*Sam nodded, watching the growing clouds and knowing he needed to get back before they broke. 'Not enough people know this country well enough to give a damn about it, don't you think?' he said. 'Cosmic yuppies communing with Mother Earth. Kids who'd be just as happy working in Alaska or Utah or Texas. No, sorry, not "working."*

*"Finding fulfillment." Like it's a goddamn church we saved just for them.'*

*Ben watched the clouds, too, confused, trying to find an ulterior motive in Sam's talk. They're naturally suspicious, these people, and talking with an outsider only makes that worse. You've seen it.*

*'Hey! You could work for me!' Sam slipped it out casual, as if it had just occurred to him.*

*'Just like that?' Ben said.*

*'Sure. You know the place,' Sam said. 'You care about it. You're smart. You're perfect, don't you think?'*

*Sam said he could see Ben's wheels turning. Ben wanted it, alright. But he was suspicious. The number two man in the Park wouldn't drive all that way to offer a random stranger a job. Of course, Sam had every right to be suspicious, too. Ben was perfect for the job and showed up at just the right time. Sam shouldn't have been so trusting.*

*The clouds were still massing, Sam said, and he needed to go. He tossed his empty beer bottle into the boat. 'Think about it. Here's my card.' He flipped aside his untucked shirttail to get his wallet. That little 9-mil he always carried hung in its nylon sheath at the center of his waistband.*

*You can just see Ben going sheet-white and goose-bumpy in a heartbeat.*

*'You could have shot me. Before,' Ben said. Then the lights went on in Ben's head. 'You knew I was out here. And who I was. Am.'*

'Told you you're smart!' Sam slapped him on the shoulder. "With you on the team, we're unbeatable.' He dropped into the boat and gunned the outboards, cutting off Ben's reply. 'I'll see you tomorrow. My office. After lunch.' Sam roared downstream, leaving Ben to sort out the offer.

Things would have been fine if that's where it ended, if Ben had just gone back to work and finished the decking. But the afternoon rain squalls broke then, washing out all sorts of junk from back in the mangrove roots where high tide had pushed it.

Ben leaned out and scooped up a Pabst can half-filled with muck. More trash lay just beyond his reach. Easing out on the mangrove roots, he grabbed more beer cans, chip bags, a pair of panties and a mud-caked pair of jeans. When he turned out the jeans pockets, out fell some coins, a soggy box of Marlboros and a plastic driver's license.

Ben picked up the license, thinking it would pay off in spades with Sam. Then he saw Henry Moton's photo staring back at him.

Ben and Henry went way back. So did their families, no matter what kind of hostilities they supposedly had. There was no way he would turn on Henry. You know these people – 'I and my cousin against the stranger.'

That's when he crossed the line. Though with James Gates for a father, I suppose it was inevitable. He slipped the license in his pocket, in that instant betrayed Sam as sure as if he'd stabbed him in the back. As sure as he tried to finish Henry's work, burned the Park 10 years later.

Ben knew if he said nothing, the chickee burning would get chalked up to unknown vandals. Honest taxpayers would pick up the tab, and Henry Moton would walk away with no one the wiser.

Before it was over two nights later, he and Henry were thick as thieves with their Mangrove Underground. How else would Ben have known where to find Henry Moton and James Gates so quickly? And why else would he have been out there with them, setting fire to half the county?

Sam was a saint through it all – gave Ben the benefit of the doubt, kept him on at the Park despite our warnings. For years it seemed like his trust was justified.

Until the burnings started again.

Until we found Ben Gates was right in the middle of them, as well.

Until Ben pinned the blame on Sam, then vanished. I hope someone did get to him. Little rat. He deserved no better.

You'll never hear that side of the story around here, though. Not with all these people covering for each other. And that desperate for heroes to worship.

## 7

The pilot nodded to Ben and jerked his thumb toward the cargo door. Ben scrambled up and strapped himself into a jump seat. The pilot tapped the side of his helmet then jabbed his finger at a headset hanging from the bulkhead next to Ben. Ben nodded, slipped the earpieces over his head, and adjusted the mike until it was almost touching his lips.

"You the big boss?" The pilot's voice crackled in his ears. Ben fumbled for the volume control by his ear.

"Assistant to the associate chief bottle washer. Ben Gates, Parks."

"Roger that. Dale Jaeger, U.S. Army." He tapped his helmet again. "You use these sets before?"

Ben's volume knob had no effect. "Yeah, but quieter."

"Uh-huh. I got your audio switch up here, at my feet. You can't transmit unless I switch it on. Talk all you want, no one'll hear you."

"Got it," Ben said.

"... flip it back and forth as we talk. I forget and leave it off and you need to ask something, tap me on the shoulder. Roger?"

"Roger dodger!"

Jaeger grinned over his shoulder. Gold captain's bars flashed on the front of his helmet. "Hang on, buckaroo."

A lurch forward, a brief grinding and they were skimming low over the smoke. Ben's stomach rolled for a moment. They banked hard left, circled the dike once, then leveled off 300 feet above the cord grass. Ben was pressed against the bulkhead as they turned again and accelerated. Through the open cargo door he saw nothing but blue sky, brown grass and the glint of sunlight on pools of water. For a moment the fires, press briefings, Kelly didn't exist.

"Need to check today's burn, huh?" Jaeger's voice exploded in Ben's ears.

"Any way to turn this thing down?" Ben pulled one earpiece away from his head.

"Huh? Oh, you get used to it." Jaeger's laughter crackled like burning leaves. The voice was so loud Ben had a hard time understanding the man. His head hurt. His stomach churned. The helicopter reeked of jet fuel and something else. Gasoline, or burned Styrofoam, maybe. Like when his dad used to throw drink cups in the fire when they went camping. Ben gritted his teeth, willed his lunch to stay down. Ahead, past Jaeger's shoulder, the smoke was still spreading.

"How far to the site?" No reply. He tapped Jaeger on the shoulder.

"Yeah, boss?"

"How far?"

"Eighteen, maybe twenty klicks. Nice, tight pattern today. Fucking beautiful. All over creation yesterday. I'll run you end-to-end."

"You fly every day?"

"Yeah, man."

"Ever see anyone down there?"

"Uh uh. No chance. Zone's always clean when we drop."

"No, before. Any sign of people down there that might be starting these things? Boats, huts, smooshed-down trails in the grass?"

Jaeger faced straight ahead, silent. Ben tapped his shoulder. No reply. He tapped again.

"Yes sir?" The headset crackled to life.

"Ever any sign of people down there?"

Silence again. Then, "You say you're with HQ, sir?"

"Yeah. Assistant super." Had he offended the man?

"Look. I'm not pointing fingers. Y'all know your jobs. I'm just making sure we haven't overlooked anything. It must have broken out right underneath you today."

"Uh huh. Hard to see where the bull gator sleeps, sir."

"A bull gator? What?" The static in the headset made understanding impossible.

"Nothing, sir. We're about there. Once around do you?"

"Probably not. Can we get around the eastern edge, see where it started?"

"Roger, sir. Only enough fuel for one pass, though."

"What happened to 'end-to-end?'" No reply.

The world turned brown, choking for a moment, then they were through the smoke and over the charred flats. A blackened scar stretched north as far as Ben could see. Out the cargo door the line of wind-driven flames ate across the marsh, widening the swath of burned ground. Clumps of cypress and water oaks smoldered, sending up darker plumes from within the burn. To the right was a wavering line where scorched earth met unburned cord grass, spared by the westerly wind. Far ahead, within the charred corridor, a thicker cloud of black smoke rose from a grove of oaks on a large hummock standing separate from the others. Tophet's Mound. Had to be. The only isolated high ground that big anywhere near. There was an old Forestry hut there, or had been. A good base for someone who knew the area. The helicopter swung right, toward the unburned grass. Ben stared at the pattern.

"The way it's scalloped out, looks almost regular," Ben said. "Somebody lit a line of something down there. Airboat, maybe?"

Silence. He tapped Jaeger's shoulder, not sure if the switch was off or if the man was ignoring him.

"Go ahead."

"Any idea what would burn a line like that?"

"Wind does some amazing things, sir."

"You set down long enough for me to get some samples? Check for accelerants?" Ben fumbled through his pockets for the resealable plastic bags he had grabbed before he left Cypress City.

"No can do, sir. Nothing to set down on."

"How about the hummock up ahead?"

"Uh uh. Still hot."

"You can lower me. Or drop me off."

"Negative, sir. Sightseeing only today."

"OK. How about a fly-by?"

"Negative. Fuel's low, sir. Gotta head back."

"Captain, why are you making this so damn difficult?"

The Blackhawk banked hard, back toward the fires. Ben clutched the frame of the canvas jumpseat to keep from tumbling out the open cargo door. They leveled out, orange flames and brown smoke framed in the cockpit's canopy.

"What the..." Ben stopped, poked Jaeger in the shoulder. "What the hell are you doing?"

"Your people'll have to run you out, sir. Later."

Ben looked over the pilot's shoulder at the dials and gauges, scanning the instrument panel. He poked Jaeger again. "You got half a tank of fuel, pal. That's got to be enough..."

Jaeger's voice crackled through the headset, cutting Ben off. "Time I drop you and get back to base, I'm on fumes. CO's gonna chew my ass as it is."

"No way you can..."

"Turbulence!" Jaeger cut in again. "Hang on! Sir."

They dropped, nose down, then lifted up again as they crossed the fire line. The helicopter slewed left then snapped back. Ben's stomach lurched with the copter. The sun slid back and forth across the canopy, sending shadows

68

careening through the cockpit. Jaeger's hands tensed on the controls as he compensated. Ben leaned back in the jumpseat, pressed himself against the padded bulkhead, breathing shallow. The pulse of the rotors slackened. The floor and seat dropped from beneath him. The floor tilted, tossing him forward, then his knees slammed into his chest as the Blackhawk pulled up. Ben tucked his upturned fire helmet between his feet, lowered his head, and vomited.

"How we holding up back there?" The voice lanced through the headset. Ben glanced at the back of Jaeger's flight helmet. The copter side-slipped right. Ben lowered his head again. "Rough ride all the way back," Jaeger's voice crackled. Ben swore the pilot was laughing. He pulled the headset off and tossed it across the cargo bay.

Twenty minutes later the bucking and rolling stopped. The whine of the rotors slackened. Ben looked out the cargo door. They were on the ground. A blue sign planted in front of the old Moton homestead proclaimed, 'Gateway to the Wilderness Coast' in white letters shaded to look three-dimensional. Below was the green-and-brown Park seal. Cypress City. Park headquarters. The asphalt parking lot, usually dotted with motor homes and rented convertibles, was packed with satellite trucks, multicolored TV news logos plastered across them. A St. Augustine grass lawn stretched between the helicopter and the parking lot. Ben tried to stand, dropped to his knees, and crawled to the door.

"Ben? You've looked better!"

Sam Archer's flushed moon-face grinned through the

doorway. Dark green canvas jacket, sleeves creased, over a light blue button-down shirt, as if no fires existed. Starched cuffs slipped from inside the jacket sleeves as Archer reached to help him down.

"Hey, boss." Ben glanced at Jaeger. The pilot was grinning. "Rough trip."

"Good. Suck it up now. Cameras are rolling." Sam slid an arm around Ben's shoulders and half-pulled him from the helicopter.

"I still have a job?"

"For now," Sam hissed. "Show your best face, Ben." Sam ducked his head under Ben's arm to support him. He grinned past Ben. "What wild hair took you out there? As if I didn't know."

"Had to see." He stumbled on a root, something. Sam's fingers dug into his ribs and held him up.

"You *have* to be here. In your office. Not tying up emergency equipment." Sam's grin didn't waver. "We need every machine we can get to keep the press grounded, off the roads. 'Closed Airspace' doesn't mean anything to *them*." The Blackhawk's blades droned louder as it lifted off, rotor wash blasting over the two men. Sam waved at the retreating copter, then turned his grin back to Ben. "You're supposed to *handle* the press, not give 'em footage. We can use this, though. Keep it light. It's showtime!"

Ahead, a wave of people, cameras and microphones surged toward them. Ben recognized some of the reporters from the past few days, but their numbers had doubled overnight. The few familiar faces were quickly lost in the mass of jeans, khaki shorts, golf shirts, canvas vests, and running shoes roiling across the lawn. To the side, photographers stood, or knelt, faces obscured by black cameras and telephoto lenses. Behind them a line of tripod-mounted television cameras stood on the asphalt. Ben tried to focus on one person, one feature until his legs obeyed him and the lawn stopped tilting. It was no use. They were on him, a blur of mouths, voices, microphones, strobes. The voices, faces, questions merged. Ben retreated into the phrases he had been repeating all week, answering what snatches of questions he could pull from the mix.

"Fire's contained... No, another flare up west of there. Closer to town, but under control... We have the best people, with the best training, doing everything they can... No, no structures, no lives lost... Marsh fires don't always make sense... Herding it away from town... Natural process in the life cycle of a swamp. Clears way for new growth."

Sam, grinning and nodding, propelled Ben through the crowd. His fingers dug deeper into Ben's ribs after each response. The crowd swirled behind him and followed, drawn along in Ben's slipstream. He tried to smile.

A face loomed among the crowd, strangely familiar, bearded, with blazing blue eyes. Ben knew the eyes. But who? From where? He slowed, locked on the face. Archer yanked his arm. Questions peppered him like buckshot. The face was gone.

"No, no increased urgency... I'm fully trained and we can always use the manpower... G-a-t-e-s... Thirty-three next month... Got a little too close. Left it in good hands, though... We have the best crews around."

They reached the asphalt and the crowd thinned. Sam was still propelling them toward the headquarters building, but not fast enough.

"No... No evidence of paramilitary camps... No evidence of marijuana cultivation... Farm runoff...?"

"More than likely." Sam broke in, pulling harder on Ben's ribs as he quickened their pace on the smooth parking lot. "We've been concerned about that for a while. But given our reduced funding and the agriculture lobby's clout, well... It's a shame it takes a wake-up call like this to show people how the environment's deteriorated. Our warnings have been falling on deaf ears for years. Now we're to the point of sending administrators out, risking their lives to stop mud and water from burning. *Mud and water!*"

They were across the parking lot then and up the headquarters' stone steps. Sam led Ben along the side of the building, pulled open a door marked 'private', and swung Ben inside.

"We'll keep everyone updated as we get more information," Sam said and closed the door behind them.

Ben collapsed on the worn cloth couch. He leaned his head back against the wall, shut his eyes to block the fluorescent glare and tried to control his stomach spasms. Dry, chilled air. No smoke. A few minutes like this and he would be fine.

"What the hell kind of stunt was that?" Sam leaned over him. "Kelly's a distinct hazard to your employment, you know that?"

"Someone's setting them," Ben whispered. The walls, ceiling, Sam's face spun. Ben pressed both arms across his stomach. "It's not runoff."

"You let me worry about that, damn it! We're on the same team! That a difficult concept?"

"The Guard pilot knows something."

*"Is that a difficult concept?"*

If he breathed just right, slow and shallow, the room would settle. "No." Ben closed his eyes again.

"Ben, we play together, we can beat this thing." Sam's voice was calmer now, a friend offering advice. "People start hot-dogging, we're sunk. I call the pitches, you play shortstop, cut everything off. You with me?"

"What happens when someone torches center field?"

"*I* handle it! You play your position, damn it!" Sam's footsteps receded. The metal desk boomed with his kick. Ben looked up. Sam spun, red-faced, finger jabbing. "You're out there playing hero, no one's here stroking Jimmy Olsen and Company. They're all up my backside today about this arson angle! You been talking to anyone besides Kelly and the entire U.S. Army?"

"No. You and Kelly. And she brought it up."

"I bet she did. And you know nothing about this?" Archer pointed to his desk. Usually well-ordered, it was strewn with loose papers. File folders lay on the floor beside open drawers. "If you hadn't been gone all day, you *might* be out of a job. Your friend Kelly, too."

"What were they looking for?"

"Who the hell knows." Archer's eyes narrowed as he watched Ben. "Proof of an arson investigation, I suspect. Now that *that* theory's out of the bag."

"It is arson. I saw it. Out by Tophet's. Black smoke from some kind of accelerant."

"I know that, Ben! That's my job. *Your* job is to make sure I don't have to explain to a bunch of professional gossips why we can't catch some moron with a box of matches."

Ben tried to focus on Sam's eyes.

Sam nodded. "Army radioed it in this afternoon."

"National Guard, you mean..."

"Guard. Yeah." Sam paused, hand over his mouth. When he spoke again his voice was lower, more even. "The Guard confirmed Kelly's reports. They're asking us to step back, keep quiet until they can find out what kind of chemicalswe're dealing with. And who's using them."

"Will we?"

"For now."

"We're going to sit on this?" The room steadied. "We'll still be burning backfires, putting out stray flare-ups, keeping things contained," Sam said. "But no word of this gets out until it's over."

Something in Sam's tone rekindled Ben's suspicions. "You think it's one of us."

"Don't even start that kind of conjecture, son. Not even in private. Hell, what makes you even think something like that?"

"You said it yesterday. Now you're pitching business-as-usual."

"Ben, Ben. We leave no stone unturned, but we're focused on the Guard right now. That and our own credibility."

"So ..." What was Archer saying? "We keep sending crews out, like these are natural fires, even though the Guard's warning us off, and you think it's a firefighter?"

"'Til it's all settled and we can lay things out on our terms? You bet. Then we'll have a big press conference and solve the mystery and nail the culprit to the barn door. We'll be heroes. Won't we, Ben?"

Ben shook his head. "This hits the news, we'll have a thousand eyes working for us, watching for us, calling us." "This hits the news? That's worse than saying we suspect our own. What would you tell them, son? You have anything, *right now*, besides suspicions? Photos? Video? Eyewitnesses? Suspect in custody? Any suspect at all? You need to get your ducks in a row before you go waving something like that around." Sam laid a hand on Ben's shoulder.

"Careers have been ruined over less."

"The park's burning, Sam!"

"Until we know who's burning it, we can't afford to say too much." Archer paused. "Hell, Ben, what if it is one of us? We'd have to present that just right. It could be... No, now you got me speculating. Next thing you'll have me thinking it's you, or Kelly, or Bailey."

"Bailey's in the hospital."   Kelly's *'Henry's not'*
sprang to Ben's mind again.

"I heard.  And we both know better.  But the wrong
person gets wind of that history..."  Archer shook his head.
"Hell, for all I know your buddy Henry is back.  That's the
buzz in town, you know."

"It's not any of us.  Or Henry."  Ben gritted his teeth.
He knew now what Kelly meant about Archer wearing on
her.  "That's what I'm saying, Ben.  We have as much evidence of that as anything else right now.  Soft-pedal the
arson angle until we know more.  See if we can't avoid more
of this."  He jerked his head toward the disordered desk.
"Maybe throw out Henry's name as a red herring."

"I won't lie."

"I'm not saying you should, Ben.  But Henry's a
legend, a folk hero, whether he's here, there, alive, dead,
what have you.  You know that."  Archer pulled up a folding
chair and sat facing Ben.  "People around here admire Henry.
Or the idea of Henry.  They think the only thing he did wrong
was get caught.  Hell, you've seen all the new 'Mangrove
Underground' flags in town the last few days."

"People are stupid."

"People need heroes.  That's not a bad thing."

"Lives are at risk, Sam.  Bailey Jenkins is in the hospital
and you want me to tell ghost stories?"

"*We* aren't telling anything, Ben.  We just drop the
name, casually, and let the vultures talk."  Archer leaned

closer. "You're like a son to me, Ben. I know it's a sore subject for you, but the talk's already there. We need to use that."

Ben shut his eyes, refocused on the fire, on arson, not on Sam's Henry Moton tangent. "We need to stop the fires." He clung to that, though his voice sounded thin, frail in the small room.

"The Army's there." Sam dropped his voice even lower, softened his tone. "Let them handle it, Ben. They've got more people, better equipment, and a better idea of what to look for and how to find it."

"They're lying."

"Maybe." Sam was still smiling, his voice low, lilting. "They may know things they're not telling us. But they're on our side. I have no problem following their lead. Neither should you."

Ben lowered his head, rubbed his temples. What Archer was saying made sense, but it didn't feel right. Ben pushed Henry and the Mangrove Underground aside. In their place sprung the image of Bailey Jenkins on the make-shift stretcher, unconscious from breathing God-knew-what.

"*If* we send crews out, they get haz-mat suits. If it's nasty enough to scare the Guard..."

"Haz-mat suits." Sam leaned back, looked at the ceiling. "Subtle. Let's see, when those photos get out, they'll empty the town, shut down the park, maybe even get someone at the capitol to notice. You *are* on an unemployment tear, aren't you, Ben?"

"We can't put our people out there unprotected. Without knowing what we're dealing with." He held fast to that point. He had to. He was the only protection his people had.

"That's their job!" Sam leaned close again. "Just a matter of days, hours, before we nail this guy. Or gal. The fires'll be out. The town'll be safe. After that, how we fare, how that swamp you care so much about fares, isn't so certain. It'll depend on how we present the facts. That's *my* job. And I'm pretty good at it."

Ben pushed himself from the couch. The room rocked, dimmed. He waited until his sight cleared. "They get haz-mat gear. They can suit up in a hangar or a shed or a damn tent if you want that a secret, but they will *damn-well* get protective gear."

Sam glared, jaw clenching. Then the familiar grin spread again in slow motion across the red face. "You promise to stay put and run interference on those piranhas out there?"

"If the Guard comes clean when it's over."

"Oh, no question of that." Sam squeezed Ben's shoulder. "Might be a commendation in this for you. Your little arrival out there made you the hero *du jour.* We can use that. You're our soot-faced poster boy now. Five seconds of you on *Nightline* 'll get us more supporters than any 20 politicians. Maybe even get our budget back up so we can protect this place like we need to, huh?"

Archer stood and stepped toward the door. "You get some rest now, son. And please, don't even think *about* it being one of our own people.

8

*Frank Marish, down at the* Skillet, *tells it best:*

*Those boys were crazy, sure. But unstoppable. One feeding off the other. They'd put the Gates-Moton differences aside – not that a couple of 12-year-olds gave a rip about their granddaddies' worn-out rum-runner feuds.*

*That's why no one was too surprised when they lit out together to catch the Canebrakes skunk ape. And if there was a skunk ape out there, no one doubted they'd find it.*

*Of course, no one knew Elena would blow up, sit 40 miles out and dump Lord-only-knows how much rain on us that week. Wonder they weren't washed away completely, two kids that far out in the sticks and nothing but each other to rely on through a Cat Four storm.*

*What got it started, now, was three tour-ons at the boat ramp going on about a big, smelly something trailing them through the backcountry, throwing rocks and sticks, tearing up their campsite. We laughed. Somebody's always messing with the Granola-crunchers – telling swamp tales, confiding low-and-quiet how lucky they were to get out alive.*

*Henry, though, his eyes lit up – started asking where-and-how questions like he actually believed the stories.*

*We thought he was leg-pulling the Yankees, maybe was even the one raiding campsites. But next thing we know he's talking out ways to track a skunk-ape, catch it, bring it back to town. Ben stood beside him, shaking his head, laughing, but you could see the light in his eyes, too. Where one went, the other followed.*

*Next morning they loaded a skiff with gear and headed out for the Canebrakes. They tried to talk the Barnes girl into going, too, but she had too much sense. "You know it's just a bear," she told us later, "or some drunk redneck. If it's anything." Always has had a mouth on her, that girl. Anyway, at first light they cast off from the canal behind the Gates place. The sky was all purple and red and orange that morning, with the clouds building, but those boys didn't give that a second thought. Or a first. Common sense left the building that day.*

*The way they told it, took them all day to get to the High Canebrake ground site. You know it – out on the edge of the wild cane fields. They poked around a bit, but it was getting on dark, so they settled in for the evening.*

*Henry, he was full of plans, sketching out maps in the dirt with a stick, with Ben correcting and making suggestions as he went – Henry knew that country better, but Ben always did have the clearer head.*

*They turned in for the night, but on toward morning they both sat bolt-upright, a God-awful stench nearly choking them. Both boys jumped up, grabbed flashlights, rolled out of the tent just in time to glimpse a shaggy something-or-other running off through the brush.*

*"A gimp in a gorilla suit," Henry called it later. He tore out after it, of course, with Ben behind, yelling for him to stop. There was no moon that night and branches slapped at their faces. All Henry could see was brush moving in front of him. All Ben could see was Henry's flashlight bouncing as he ran. And both of them choking on that smell, more following that than any trail they could see.*

*Then, BAM! Three things happened all at once: Ben heard a splash, Henry hollered, and his light disappeared. Ben slowed, crept up careful. The wind had blown some of the stench away and he caught a hint of the thick, woody smell of a cypress head. Water seeped in through his boots and he knew deep water was close.*

*Henry was splashing and hollering bloody murder about alligators by then. Ben followed the sound and found Henry, forehead bleeding, flailing away in the gator hole in the middle of that cypress stand. He didn't see any gators, but he wasted no time finding a branch and pulling Henry out, either.*

*Back in camp, Henry swore the skunk-ape had lured him, turned aside at the last second and run him into the sink. Ben, he said it was a bear, if a damned smelly one, and lucky it hadn't turned on them.*

*By then it was getting light. Or as light as it would get for the next few days (though they didn't know that at the time). Henry was all for tracking whatever it was, proving Ben wrong. If he was concerned about Ben having saved his life, he didn't show it. That sort of thing happened every other day with those two.*

*They said later there were mushed-down spots that could have been footprints in the mud around the campsite – big footprints, without claw marks, closer to human prints than bear prints. And in twos, not fours. Ben, he laughed, then fell in behind Henry and off they went.*

*The tracks led back toward the cypress head and disappeared in the marsh. It took those boys a while to criss-cross around the edge of the soggy land, but they finally picked up a trail leading away from the water and on toward the cane fields.*

*Henry found a clump or two of coarse black hair caught on cypress bark. Stunk to high heaven, he said – more proof of a skunk ape. Ben called it proof someone was messing with them. When Henry asked who'd be messing with them that far from anywhere, Ben said, "Someone who don't want to be found."*

*That riled Henry, you can imagine. Stuffed the hair clumps in his pocket and stomped off, following the trail. Ben followed, not believing Henry, but curious and not about to leave him alone that far out.*

*They were right in the cane by then, both boys carrying dead branches for clubs, alert for any movement and watching for the snakes that are thick in the 'Brakes. Soon the stalks were 20, 25 feet high around them, blocking out the sky. Clouds were building something fierce by then, and the rain was starting, but the boys barely noticed, they were so deep in the cane.*

*They hadn't been in the 'Brakes too long when Henry caught another whiff of skunk ape. A second later something* went crashing past, and they tore after it, running hard in spite of the gagging stench. Every now and then Henry said he caught a glimpse of something tall and shaggy lumbering ahead of them, always just at the edge of sight in the dim light and swaying stalks.

About then they realized the cane all around them was starting to shake. They couldn't see much sky or feel much wind, but they could sure feel those stalks rattling, like the two of them were fleas on a big dog scratching to get them off.

The rain kicked in hard about then, and no cane stalks, no matter how tall, could shield them from that. Henry glanced back at Ben. Ben grinned – they'd be soaked whether they went back to camp or kept on. They were hot on the trail, for better or worse, and rain be damned.

Henry and Ben kept tracking, through the dark and rain, for hours. The wind was laying the cane tops down level with their heads by then. Lightning jagged around them. Thunder boomed so loud it shook the ground. Before long the rain came down so thick they couldn't see a step in front of them, and the ground started running with rainwater.

They pushed ahead as best they could, but when they could barely see each other, they knew it was no use. They turned for camp. Thing is, they couldn't see a thing any direction except rain and thrashing cane – and that just briefly when lightning crackled. With no compass or trail to follow, camp could have been anywhere.

Henry, though, he had the swamp sense, managed to dead-reckon the general direction they needed. By then rain-

*water was running so heavy they could have been wading down a creek.*

*Lord only knows how long Henry and Ben wandered through that storm. They went on and on, into the night, with the water rising all the while, currents getting stronger, getting closer and closer to pulling them off their feet. Finally, the cane began to thin a bit, and Henry hollered out* he could make out cypress tops ahead.

*Lightning flashed.*

*RAWR! came from right behind them.*

*Ben spun just in time to see a hairy hand swat him upside the head. Laid him out, face-down, and he would have been gone right then if Henry hadn't turned back, pulled Ben's head up with one hand while he swung his club at the critter.*

*The thing reared up, Henry said, a full three feet taller than him, and roared again. It swung one paw and ripped the club from his hand so fast Henry didn't see the critter move. The stink of it like to knocked him out. Knowing he had no chance on land against something that big and that fast, Henry pulled Ben away, into deeper water. The skunk ape splashed after them, roaring so loud it drowned out the thunder. Henry had no choice but to swim, towing an unconscious Ben, and hope the skunk ape couldn't swim, too. Or that it'd drown trying.*

*The critter must have known what Henry was thinking, because it backed off knee-deep and grabbed onto a cypress trunk with one hand while it roared and clawed the air and* tore off bark and branches to throw. Henry grabbed a passing log and let the current take him and Ben away, figuring them both for dead, but not about to give up.

Neither boy could ever say how long they floated like that. We had given up finding them, what with half the county blown away. Three days later they washed up by our old place – near the ranger station down at Ibis Point, laid out on logs lashed together with bootlaces and vines. They'd gotten by on rainwater, berries that floated by, and what Henry called 'drowned fish.' (He swore it rained that hard, and I about believed him – Elena took out most of the town before she moved on.)

We never did find their skiff, or their gear. Or any more sign of the skunk ape. Henry hung onto the clumps of hair, though. For a while he'd bring them out, pass them around whenever someone doubted his story, but after a few years he gave them to the Heritage Museum, which sent them on up to the university.

Scientists up there never could tell what kind of hair it was, or from what kind of critter. Ben swore it was a bear that whacked him, but there was always a little catch in his voice when he said it. All I can speak to is there were no claw marks where that thing hit his head. And not too many bears stand on their hind legs and hang onto trees while they throw sticks at folks.

Tree huggers and locals alike stayed clear of the Canebrakes after that, and even so there were still stories of some big something trailing people through other parts *of the swamp, stinking to high heaven. Still are, from time to time.*

*That's a comfort. Keeps folks looking over their shoulders, respectful of the deep swamp. Reminds us we're never as strong or as smart as we think we are.*

## 9

The oak ceiling fan at the Three Hounds Hunt Club spun in front of Ben, blurred, coalesced into individual blades, then blurred back into a circular smudge obscuring the ceiling panels 20 feet above the table. To either side, where the varnished oak walls angled from the corner, the heads of boar, bear, and bighorn sheep loomed over him. Directly above, as far back as his upturned eyes could roll, a silver tarpon arched six feet toward a Thompson's gazelle's tan chin.

Ben closed his eyes, felt the fan wash away the remnants of burned cord grass he hadn't been able to scrub off in a hot shower. He rested his hands on the chair arms and stretched his legs under the table. Voices floated around him – conversations in the lounge, a few whoops from the bar in the next room. The pre-dinner crowd, or fans in to catch a football game on TV. A rum and Coke sat on the table somewhere in front of him, but taking a sip would have meant moving, sitting up. He pushed the drink from his mind and tried to make each muscle in his head relax.

It didn't make sense. He wanted to believe Sam, make the facts mesh neatly with the National Guard's story, but he couldn't. Not for more than a few seconds. Sam said the Guard was tracking the culprit. That part was fine. But why had the Guard pilot been so evasive? Were they tracking a rogue Guardsman? Some former-military type? That could be why they closed their base to civilians. Or was it a civilian firefighter, and the Guard didn't want to tip off Forestry?

Had Ben's, or Kelly's, connection to Henry Moton's lunacy years before drawn attention? The basic events were common knowledge, though most details never came out. The story had grown, changed with retelling, though. Ben's name could have set Jaeger off. But Sam would have cleared that up quickly... if the Guard had mentioned it.

Ben took a deep breath and unclenched his jaws. In less than a minute he had gone from logic, to paranoia, to guilt, revisiting events he had put far behind him. His stomach tightened as hard as it had at the barge 10 years before. He had failed then, failed himself, his family and his friends. But that was a lifetime ago and had nothing to do with what was happening now.

With these fires, Sam's story didn't jibe with Jaeger's actions. A bureaucratic miscommunication, maybe, with the Guard and the Park not trusting each other? Ben hoped it was that simple. All he knew for sure was that Kelly and her people were being thrust into danger, and they were all being kept in the dark, even Sam. The Guard's explanation didn't make sense. No, he corrected himself – he had heard only Sam's explanation. He didn't have enough information, and his imagination was filling in the gaps. This was paranoia again, suspecting Sam Archer of double-dealing with his own people. Sam was tough. Sam didn't play fair. But Sam didn't burn his own.

Cheers boomed from the next room. Several people dog-barked in unison. Ben opened one eye, keeping his head relaxed. Four men in dark green flight suits had wandered in, their clothes and close-cropped hair setting them apart from the tourists and locals watching the game. He didn't see Jaeger. Lying bastards. But Sam knew it. Ben realized that now. Sam was playing along until he had more facts. It was classic Sam: divert attention and work an angle. Probably a semi-legal one. Even so, Ben trusted Sam more than the Guard. Sam's motives were convoluted, but he meant well. No matter what Kelly or anyone else said.

She had been furious years before when documents mysteriously appeared at Park headquarters showing produce and mining companies were illegally dumping chemicals upstream from the Park. "He stole them," Kelly had said. Sam publicly thanked the 'concerned citizen' who had left the documents. Lawyers were still arguing the legality of the find, but public outrage had stopped the dumping. "He wins like that, eventually he'll lose like that," Kelly had said. "We all will."

"But he's pro-Park. Pro-environment," Ben had said. "No," she said, "he's pro-Sammy."

Now, in the lounge, Ben stifled a laugh. Henry Moton had been credited with stealing those documents as well.

Ben stared at the swirling fan blades. Until he knew more, going along with Sam was his only option. Sam was one of the good guys. Ben would dig deeper, safeguard the fire crews, and let Sam worry with the bigger picture. Ben's throat tightened thinking of his flight back that morning. Sam was right – Ben might have spoiled things already.

"Follow through, Ben." He mimicked Kelly's voice. The whispered words swirled away in the fan's draft.

"Talking to yourself. Not a good sign." Metal-tipped chair legs screeched across the hardwood floor to his right.

Ben winced and sat up. "Hey, Kel."

She was freshly showered. Her braided ponytail, dark with water, stained the shoulder of her khaki shirt. She leaned forward on the table, fingers laced around a green beer bottle.

Ben met her gaze, not sure how to react. She would want to know what happened on the helicopter, but their morning face-off was still fresh in his mind. And all the talk of Henry had reopened old wounds. Ben waited for her to speak, to see which way the conversation would go.

"Look, I'm sorry. About this morning." Her voice trailed away, lost in the noise spilling from the bar.

"No problem," Ben said. "Bad situation."

"No, I shouldn't have blown up. Not in front of everyone." She leaned closer, eyes locked on Ben's. "I just came from the hospital. Bailey's touch-and-go. He inhaled a lot of smoke."

Ben nodded.

"What'd you find?"

Ben started to speak, then stopped, suspicious. It was crazy to think Kelly had anything to do with these fires, but the doubt was there. She had helped Henry. And what better way to find out how close the pursuit was than to ask the pursuers?

"Ben?"

"I don't know." Ben sat silent again. He needed someone to trust, talk it out with, see if they could make sense of things. But could he trust Kelly? She was still staring at him. "Sam's threatening me in one breath, then stroking me the next. But I still have a job. I'm supposed to make nice with the press and let him find the firebug."

Kelly smiled. "You found the points of ignition, didn't you?"

Ben watched her face for any out-of-place expression. No, he was crazy. This was Kelly. He had no logical reason to doubt her.

"In a nice, neat line. The guy wouldn't land, but Sam knows they're being set. Says the Guard told him this morning."

*"Says?"*

"The Guard found traces of some funky accelerants. Maybe military stuff, so they're calling the shots until they have more to go on. For now, we deal with the fires as they break out."

Kelly watched him, expressionless, for so long he thought she hadn't heard. He started to speak, but she held up a hand.

"They think it's one of us." There was no question in her voice. "What does Sammy say?"

"Play along. Ride it out. Don't talk to strangers." Ben studied her, still debating how much to tell her.

"Ohhh, don't trust him, Ben. He's... he thinks it's me. Doesn't he?" Her eyes narrowed. "He planted that in your head!"

"If I thought it was you, we wouldn't be talking about this, would we?"

"I'm gonna... no, there's no way for me to talk to him about this without sounding guilty. Or getting you fired. Nice. He has you fishing for him, whether you know it or not. He's a snake!"

"But he's *our* snake. And the one person with the stroke to do something about this, since the Guard won't talk to you or me."

"The man cultivates fall-guys, Ben. He'll cut you and watch you bleed. He's done it to others."

Ben paused. Who had Sam set up? And when? It didn't matter. He ignored it and went on. "Tomorrow you get haz-mat suits. And I'll keep digging."

Kelly leaned back in her chair. "He's made you the perfect spokesman – you don't know anything, you can't let anything slip." She spun the sweating beer bottle in front of her, then picked at the paper label without looking at it. "Do they really think it's one of us? It could just as easily be one of them, especially if Sammy's not making up that stuff about the accelerants."

"What do you have against him, anyway?" It was out before he realized it. He shouldn't be annoyed with her, he knew, but he was.

Kelly hesitated, her eyes locked on his for several seconds before she spoke. "You're *still* hung up on me and Henry, aren't you?"

"Kelly, that has nothing to do with..."

"Uh huh. And I'll bet Sammy mentioned Henry – in passing – about the same time he hinted at me setting fires. He's muddying the water, Ben, making sure your judgment's good and clouded."

Ben's face felt hot, numb. "We buried all that a long time ago." Her fling with Henry had been brief. And long ago.

"Then act like it." Kelly could have been reading his mind. "Why would Sammy be so interested in us doubting each other, Ben? What would he gain by that?"

"Why does this have to be about Sam?"

"I... don't know what's going on any more than you do. But I do know we have to trust each other. I do trust you, Ben."

Kelly reached across the table and took his hand. Ben froze. They hadn't touched for years. Not like this. She smiled. "We're friends, right? Or close to it?"

Ben forced himself not to react. Even blinking would have upset the balance he fought to maintain. He didn't love her. Not anymore.

"OK, still working on 'friends,'" Kelly said. "But we can trust each other in this. Right?"

Ben slid his hand from hers, slowly, trying not to seem too abrupt. Part of him wanted to sit like this with her again, or feel it was an option. But the old anger, guilt, the blame flared up inside him. Ben let his vision blur so he could speak to a vague shape rather than to Kelly herself.

"I trust you. But..." Ben paused again, watching his hands tighten on themselves, not wanting to argue with her. "I'm not stupid. I know Sam. I also know what I'm doing. Just... I know what I'm doing."

"Ben, when you carried Bailey through those flames, when you climbed into that helicopter today, I was so proud of you. It was the old Ben. Him I'd trust with my life."

Ben's head snapped up, more at her tone than her words. There was sincerity there, an honesty he had cherished, an intensity he had loved. Kelly stared back at him.

"You're always so close to being the person you could be, Ben. I want to help, but you have to make that last step yourself."

Ben's face burned. A decade of buried thoughts, emotions burned through him again. He stared past Kelly, seeing nothing. His jaws hurt. He wanted to speak, but the words wouldn't come. He closed his eyes, took a deep breath. "I'm trying to do what's right. For everyone. Especially you." The pain surged back, as sharp as ever.

Kelly took his hand again. "I don't matter, Ben. Neither do you. Neither do stupid mistakes we made as kids. The only thing that matters is there's something very wrong going on, and you have the chance to do something about that."

"What? Break into the Armory? Kidnap a pilot and rough him up?" The words were out before he realized it. Kelly pulled away.

"Sam's lying to you. Bailey's in ICU with tubes down his throat. One Guard pilot stonewalled you. You ever think of talking to any other pilots?" It was the angry Kelly of that morning, counting off points on her fingers. "And yeah, getting into the Armory might be a good thing."

Yells from the bar came so loud he could barely hear her. Several people, including the soldiers, were making chomping motions with their arms.

"Look, Ben. There's some Guard pilots in the bar. I wonder if they might shed light on any of this?"

"I promised Sam I wouldn't mess with the Guard if he got you haz-mat suits."

"Try this, Ben: 'Ooops! Sorry Sam. I screwed up!' Anyway, you're not working, are you? You just ran into them at the bar. I was here. Saw the whole thing."

"You weren't in that chopper this morning, Kel. I talk to them now, knowing nothing, I could screw things up."

"More than things already are? I'm sure they'd talk with a top-dog Park supervisor who's in on things and all."

He was angry, as angry as she was. But she was right. He did trust her, he realized. He surprised himself by saying, "Yeah, they might."

"They might even give you a ride up to the Armory, let you see something even Sammy doesn't know about.

What do you have to lose?"

"My job..." Kelly glared. "Yeah." He stood and hugged her quickly, stiffly, stumbling against the table. "Thanks, Kel." Ben walked toward the bar, his body feeling lighter with each step, as if invisible air tanks and asbestos jacket were being stripped from him as he walked. He wouldn't let her down. He wouldn't let any of them down.

Inside the bar people stood in clusters, faces raised toward several ceiling-mounted televisions. At the near end of the bar, the four men in olive drab jumpsuits were chanting it was 'great to be a Florida Gator,' waving mugs of beer over their heads like boys playing with toy airplanes. Ben reached through the cluster of pilots and slapped a ten dollar bill on the bar in front of the bartender. "Keep the change," he yelled. He stepped back and slapped the nearest pilot between the shoulder blades. "Dale! How you doing, buddy!" The pilot staggered forward then caught himself on the bar with his free hand. He turned to face Ben, the arm of his flight suit soaked halfway to the elbow with beer. The other pilots stepped back.

"You suicidal, Sparky?" Lieutenant's bars glinted on his shoulders.

"Oh, man, my mistake." Ben reached for a stack of napkins. Boots shuffled behind him, cutting off any retreat. "You looked like a friend of mine. Dale Jaeger from up at the Armory?" He held the napkins out to the pilot.

"Your mistake. That it is." The lieutenant set his near-empty beer mug on the bar without looking.

Ben realized he was looking up at the man. The pilot outweighed him by at least 50 pounds.

"Hey, I'm sorry. Can I buy you another?"

"I liked the one I had."

"I'll buy you two. Coors?"

The pilot hesitated. Feet shuffled closer behind Ben, almost at his heels. "No, it was a Heineken." He glanced at the bartender. "Two of them, on Smokey the Bear's tab." He turned back to Ben. "I never drink that cheap domestic stuff." Boots scuffled behind Ben again, this time moving toward the bar and away from the door.

"Can't blame you," Ben said. "Rough day?"

The lieutenant, 'Ferry' according to his uniform, studied Ben. "How you know Captain Jaeger?"

"We've been working together. Closed this place down a few nights back."

"The Captain was here? Good to know."

"Why?"

"City's off-limits. We're rolling dice, but it's the only place to get the Florida-Georgia game." Ferry grinned. "Of course, we get busted now, Captain can't nail us too hard. Thanks for the heads-up."

"You bet." Ben hoped his laugh didn't sound too forced. Ferry didn't seem to notice. "I was hoping he'd be here this evening."

"He owe you money?"

"No, no. Nothing like that. I need a lift. There's some big-wig meeting at the Armory. The boss'll skin me if I'm not there. No way I can drive there in time."

"Three minutes of game time left, and we're out of here," Ferry said. "But the base is closed to civilians."

"Like the bar's closed to pilots?"

Ferry grinned. "That could get me busted. Big-time. Without authorization, or checking if it's slick with the C.O. ..."

A phrase of Jaeger's buzzed in Ben's head, a phrase that had puzzled him all afternoon. It was worth a try. "You mean if I knew where bull gators sleep?"

"Where the sun don't shine!" Ferry grinned and drained his beer mug. "That works! Now *please* don't tell me you're a Bulldog fan."

## 10

*Judge George Barnes generally had a feel for people:*

*James Gates was a good man, financial malfeasance and narcotics trafficking notwithstanding.*

*His defining moment, to my mind, wasn't his trial and conviction, but rather our first meeting 10 years before, when he drove his son out directly from the principal's office, marched him up to our front door and ensured he apologized properly.*

*To this day I'm not certain whether he was more concerned with family honor, with Ben's personal culpability, or with Kelly's injury.*

*Were I to offer conjecture, it would be at-odds with the popular images of James Gates the Populist Demagogue declaiming at length in commission sessions, or the Unrepentant Public Official funding his crimes with local tax monies.*

*James brought Ben by that afternoon because he saw it as the right thing to do.*

*"What you meant doesn't matter, Ben," he told his son. "It's what you do says who you are. And what you did ... we're lucky she wasn't hurt worse."*

*This was long before James entered politics, you understand. Long before I had to sentence him. I was a lowly public defender at the time, he was an even lower commercial waterman. Janet and I had just come to Cypress City – Kelly and Ben couldn't have been more than 10 or 11. Janet answered the door that day and glanced from Ben to James standing with his arms crossed at the edge of the porch, waiting for one of the Gates men to speak.*

*Kelly intervened, as usual. She stepped from behind her mother and glared at Ben, her eye swollen nearly shut. "What are you doing here?" she said.*

*Ben apologized, penitent, eyeing his feet as he spoke. "Sorry I hit you this morning. I didn't mean to, but it was wrong. What can I do to make up for it?"*

*There was an uncomfortable silence after he finished. Janet broke that by sending both kids out back and inviting James Gates inside to talk.*

*Ben's temper had bested him at recess that morning. I believed him when he said he'd meant Kelly no harm. But that didn't change what had happened, or absolve him of self-given guilt. For years you could see it when he'd squeeze his arms across his stomach whenever someone – usually Kelly – mentioned it.*

*Henry Moton had been the catalyst, naturally, taunting Ben, calling him weak and a sissy. Kelly's head simply was in the wrong spot when Ben spun and threw the ball as hard as he could into the dodge ball ring.*

*Amanda Morehouse said Kelly hit the ground before the ball did. She also said Ben was kneeling beside Kelly before anyone else could move, begging her to be all right, begging her to speak.*

*Henry Moton exacerbated the situation, though he quickly regretted it. One moment he was slapping Ben on the back, congratulating him on welcoming the new girl to Briar Patch Elementary, the next he was on the ground himself, with Ben grinding his face into the dirt and punching with his free hand. As if the Gates and Motons needed anything more to fight about.*

*That may have been why James Gates was so intent on Ben making amends with all concerned. Delmore Moton was one to reciprocate any transgressions against his family, and brawling with one of his boys would have been an affront to Moton family dignity. Or what passed for it.*

*Whatever the reason, James sipped tea with Janet in the living room for more time than was strictly necessary, volunteering to pay any medical bills and offering Ben's services for any yard work or cleaning we needed done. Janet said he spent much of the conversation staring out the picture window, to where Ben and Kelly sat at the edge of the back yard, watching for signs they had resolved their differences.*

*I saw that same quality in him time and again when he was on the zoning board, and later the county commission. He would nudge adversaries in the appropriate direction, but always allow them room to assuage the differences themselves.*

*In retrospect, I don't think he, Janet, or anyone else had any clue those two kids would connect like they did. And continued to do, right to the end, despite all the bumps they put each other through along the way. For better or worse, they were joined from that day forward.*

*What James saw that afternoon was Kelly leading Ben down to the water, the St. Augustine grass folding over their feet as they crossed the lawn. At the seawall Kelly leaned one-footed, like she does still, against one of the davits, studying Ben.*

*Ben stood opposite, stiff. He had apologized, as his father had asked. As he had on the playground, and again in the nurse's office. "I really am sorry," he finally said.*

*Kelly said she tried to smile, but her bruised face turned that into a grimace. "Sorry I hit you with my lunch box," she said.*

*"I think your thermos broke," Ben said, and rubbed the top of his head.*

*"Yeah." Kelly nodded. "Mom was mad. It's OK, though."*

*Ben folded his arms across his stomach and stared downriver. Four miles that direction, across the causeway, was his home. The afternoon breeze, full of the low-tide smells of fish and mud flats, swirled through the rips in his shirt. Ben sat on the seawall, feet dangling over the water,* and leaned forward over folded arms. Kelly sat next to him, waiting for him to speak.

"You from up north?" he finally said.

Kelly laughed at that. "Sort of. Atlanta."

"Oh," Ben said. He bounced his heels on the cement, as if testing its solidity.

"We used to come here on vacation. So my dad could fish," Kelly said. "Then he bought this place, and we moved down. He says so he can walk out the back door, get in his boat and fish whenever he wants – that's where he is now." She watched him for a moment, then asked, "You live on the water, too?"

Ben nodded without looking at her. "On the island." He waved a hand downriver, toward Catahoula Key. "But everyone has docks there."

"Oh, that's so much better than a stupid sea-wall!" Kelly said, in her way. "You can see all kinds of fish underneath a dock!"

Ben shrugged. "Snappers and stuff. At night, with a lantern, there's barracuda, snook, sometimes nurse sharks."

"I would love that," Kelly said. "Sometimes I lie on my stomach out here and imagine I'm a fish, gliding through the water. You ever do that?"

"A fish?" Ben finally looked at her, but as though she was crazy.

"You never imagine you're a fish?"

"No."

"Really?" Kelly said. "I'd love to be a fish – that

*free and graceful. I'd be a.... a..."*

"Squirrelfish?" Ben flinched as he said it, as though he hadn't meant to speak aloud. He stared down at the water, at the clouds reflected on the surface, unable to withdraw the remark.

Kelly scooted closer, though, bouncing her heels in time with his. "I thought maybe a queen angelfish... you know, all black and blue?" She waited for a reaction. Ben squeezed his ribs tighter. Kelly laughed.

"It's OK," she said when he still refused eye contact. She put a hand on his shoulder. "Thanks for your jacket. I don't think I got any blood on it."

Ben looked up at that. "I really didn't mean to hurt you," he said.

"I know," Kelly said. "Thanks for coming."

"My dad made me." Ben looked away again.

"Still..." Kelly stared across the water, as if talking to the trees on the far bank. "I'm glad you came. It probably sounds weird, but I... don't know anyone here. Pretty lame, huh?"

Ben eyed the trees across the way for a moment, like he was trying to see what Kelly saw. "You're happy to see the person who knocked you out?" he said.

"We're even," she said. "Things can't get any worse between us, right?"

Ben squinted at the water. Sun on the ripples made bright-and-dark patterns that reflected up across both their faces. He held his hands in front of him, making a frame with his thumbs and fingers, as if to block out everything but the water and sunlight.

"I'm sorry, too... about your mom," Kelly said.

Ben looked away at that, his face, everything about him tense.

"They told me at school. Mrs. Walker and the nurse. I'm sorry."

"Not your fault." Ben turned back to the river, fingers framed in front of him again. Neither spoke for several minutes.

"Sometimes I sit out here and wonder where the water goes," Kelly said. "Besides the Gulf, I mean. It's like, where does light from the stars come from, you know? It starts somewhere, and it goes somewhere, but all we see is a little slice of it." She talked like that, even at that age.

Ben folded his arms across his stomach again and leaned forward, staring across the river. "Sorry," he whispered. He turned away then and rubbed a hand across his cheeks a few times. He started to get up, then settled back next to Kelly. Neither spoke. They simply sat there, watching the light play across the water, while inside, Janet and James Gates looked on.

Ben and Kelly were still there, side-by-side, when I brought the boat in at dusk.

## 11

The Blackhawk rotors pulsed steady, a deep throb Ben felt through his boot soles and the taut canvas jumpseat. The same gasoline-and-Styrofoam smell from the helicopter that morning washed around him. Through the window to his left the sun hung orange above a horizon of silhouetted palm trees.

"Dunno know what's up. Super's there already," Ben yelled into the mouthpiece. "They tell me where to go, and when, but not much else. The old 'need-to-know' routine."

"I heard that!" Lt. Ferry's voice crackled harsh, but bearable, in his ears. "Sure you're not in the Army?"

"Feels like it, sometimes."

Below, the salt marsh gave way to asphalt roads, then concrete pads and low clusters of buildings. Ferry circled the base once before angling toward a landing pad. Rows of olive-shaded helicopters ringed the cement. Fifty-five gallon fuel drums stood five high and ten deep at the edge of the pad. On the opposite side, as far from the fuel as possible, smaller, narrower canisters, half as large, lay stacked on their sides in metal racks.

"Looks like y'all are ready for Fidel to invade."

"Toast his ass back to Havana if he does."

"All that fuel?"

"The big ones, yeah. Small ones are ordnance."

"Ordnance?"

"Yeah, man. New and improved. Burns through hell and half of Florida."

Ben's stomach tightened as the Blackhawk slowed, dropped. There was more than enough below to fight 100 fires. "Kinda hard-core for backfires."

"Backfires, front fires, and any kind you got! As long as it tests to specs. How is it to control once it's lit?"

"Uh... About what you'd expect." Images, bits of conversation dove-tailed in Ben's mind. 'New and improved.' Why would the National Guard be using something like this on a backcountry fire? Unless the military wanted it tested in a real-world situation. The Guard could do what it wanted, wherever it wanted on public land, but they would have told the Park and Forestry. They had to know something like this in the Park wouldn't stay secret so close to a population center. There were too many people watching, too many television cameras. Sam would gut them.

"Didn't know the Guard had access to stuff like this," Ben said.

"Guard! Right! Like anyone knows the difference."

"Sure." Ben's stomach tightened again. "You could have fooled me."

"That's the idea." Ferry grinned.

"It... uhh... test to specs?" Ben needed to keep the man talking, distracted. "Oh yeah! Used to have to hit tropical vegetation two, three times to keep it lit. Mangroves, coca – too damn wet. This stuff, though, the... ahh, appropriate parties can toast the Huallaga Valley back to the Stone Age in one drop."

A slight bump and they were down. Ben yelled, "Thanks," slipped the headset off, and hopped to the ground, trying to look confident, like he belonged there. He wound through clusters of tied-down helicopters, toward the hangar where Ferry said the C.O.'s office was. Ben had no idea what to do next, how to get the information he needed and get himself off the base. The implications were hitting him too quickly, from unexpected directions. He didn't need Jaeger anymore. He needed evidence, samples, and a way back to Cypress City.

Cell phone at hip level as he passed the canisters, Ben photographed the writing stenciled on their sides, then a wider shot of the entire stack after he had passed.

He would get what evidence he could, try to avoid getting shot or arrested, then bluff and hope Sam could bail him out. He punched Sam Archer's number into his phone as he walked. He could send the photos now. The phone beeped. No signal this far out. Well, if he couldn't bring the evidence to Sam, maybe he could bring Sam to the evidence. But he needed something more than photos first.

Ben ducked through the partially-closed doors of an empty hangar. Fluorescent light glared off pale cinderblock walls. The scrubbed cement floor gleamed. Dark brown doors, spaced intermittently, lined the walls on three sides. Mirrored glass next to the doors on the far wall marked offices. He headed across the hangar, keeping close to the wall. A door swung open to his right.

Sam Archer stepped into the hangar, grinning, but face redder than Ben had ever seen it. "Hey, Ben, glad you could make it! You didn't have to run out personally!" His voice was too loud, too high. His eyes burned cold, bored into Ben's. He clamped a hand on Ben's upper arm. Ben winced as pain shot from his elbow to his shoulder. Sam spun Ben away from the door and window, hissed low, his voice shaking. "I'm gonna cut your balls off and feed 'em to you, you don't play right along with my lead." Sam was still grinning, but his nostrils flared with each breath. "You mouth off here, you'll *wish* you were the raw meat they throw to the dogs."

Despite the pain and Sam's threats, Ben relaxed. Sam was a step ahead of him, already checking out the base himself. Leaning on the Guard commander. *Army* commander, rather. He should have known.

"They have enough napalm, or something, to start a war," Ben whispered.

"Dick Fucking Tracy," Sam hissed. "You keep your mouth *shut*. Your job here is to be invisible unless I need a 'Yes, sir.' You got that?"

Ben nodded. Sam had leverage. The Army couldn't indiscriminately burn public land, certainly not land near homes, land full of wilderness campers. Forestry was the only agency with enough trained people to control fires like these, but they weren't at the military's disposal, any more than the Park was. Or shouldn't be... there was still something he wasn't seeing.

Sam steered him toward the bay doors, hand talon-tight on his arm. "You surprised me, Ben. Broke the rules, took the initiative. Good traits for the man in charge of the Park."

Ben slowed, trying to piece together what Sam was saying.

"You don't think I plan to be here forever, do you, Ben? As soon as we finish up this business, I'll be moving onward. Upward." Sam's smile relaxed, his voice was lower, more even.

"This business?"

"The Park'll be in great shape Ben. You played a big part in that. I won't forget it."

Ben stared, cold shooting through him. The pieces had been in there all along. The Army couldn't fire-bomb the Park unless the Park let them. Sam had to have known. But why? Sam wanted... power. Influence. No, that was too far-fetched. Sam went to extremes to protect the wilderness, but burning it... for personal gain?

"Tell me this isn't money and politics, Sam." Ben's voice was barely a whisper. His lips felt numb.

"*Everything's* money and politics, Ben. You know that." Sam's voice hissed soft, low. "A leader has to know that." He nodded toward the open office door. "If the colonel finds out you're not in on this, we can shoot ourselves right here."

"You can't..." Ben pulled back. Sam's grip tightened.

"*We* already did, partner. Or do you prefer 'official spokesman?'"

"I didn't do anything!" Ben's skin burned, as if the fires had erupted around him.

Sam nodded. "You're up to your neck in it, Ben." The grin never wavered. "Ever since you lied on camera in front of God and everyone. They call that 'felony conspiracy.' In arson. In destroying Federal property. Maybe even in manslaughter if Bailey Jenkins doesn't pull through."

Words wouldn't come. The heat was inside him now, surging up. Ben wanted to punch the grin from Sam's face, or run away, or curl up in a ball.

Sam stopped in the corner of the hangar, as far from the open office door as he could get. "Listen to me, Ben. This is the most important thing you'll ever hear. You know how you feel when you see people win against impossible odds? Good, right? They're heroes – you rush to be a part of it, share the victory. Hell, if they have a t-shirt or a jersey, you buy one."

"What are you talking about?"

"We've been short-changed on funding, supplies, and personnel for years now, Ben. But that's gonna change. In a couple of days the Park and Forestry will make a last valiant effort and stop these horrible wildfires. Within sight of the town, the press, and every television set in the country. *We'll* be the heroes. That means *lots* of warm, fuzzy feelings for the Park and the idyllic swamp. That also means they double our budget at the hearings next month. Combined, that's instant salvation from those nasty ol' developers and farms and mining companies."

"It stops today, Sam! Now! I don't care what the hell you have cooking! *We* don't destroy the land!" Ben saw himself hitting Sam, as clearly as if he had already knocked him down.

"It stops when it's served its purpose. There's nothing..."

"Everything alright, Archer?" A voice boomed through the empty hangar. Boots clopped across cement.

"Yeah, Colonel. Just sorting out some housekeeping," Sam yelled. Then a whisper to Ben, "For now we avoid... professional repercussions."

Sam turned back toward the rear of the hangar, spinning Ben with him. Ben yanked free of Sam's grip.

"They stop *now*," Ben whispered. "Or it all blows up." He tried to match Sam's grin as the walked.

"Colonel E.K. Schmitz? Ben Gates, my assistant. He's handling the press for us." Ben smiled and shook the colonel's hand. "Colonel, you have a good enough idea what that stuff of yours can do?"

"We could use another day or two." Blue eyes, level with Ben's own, locked onto his. Hair graying around the ears. Tiger-stripe fatigues. "Why?"

"Ben here says some of the media-types are asking why regular Army choppers are fighting fires." Sam's voice was velvet comfort. "Sounds like some of your boys been mouthing off at the Three Hounds."

The colonel's eyes snapped to Sam. "Bar's off-limits. So's the town."

"Yes, sir. I know. That's where Ben hopped a flight just now."

The colonel glared at Ben. Ben met his gaze but said nothing.

"These exercises are over," the colonel said. "I'll leave media control to you, gentlemen." He nodded to Sam, then to Ben. "You'll excuse me. I have some pilots to... debrief." He ducked under the hangar door and was gone.

"That good enough for you, Ben?" Sam's face was expressionless, but his eyes blazed. "Your conscience cleaner now?" He turned and followed the colonel out the door before Ben could answer.

Ben followed him around the hangar to the Park Service Taurus. Sam slid behind the wheel and opened the passenger door without looking at Ben. They drove across the base, through the gates, down the raised limerock that served as a dike and roadbed, and onto the crumbling asphalt of State Road 27, neither man speaking. They headed south, skimming level with the tops of the marsh grass. Lingering smoke streaked the orange sunset with wisps of deep umber. Like the swamp was a bed of coals, a lake of fire.

"We were that close." Sam shook his thumb and index finger at Ben. "One final rescue scene in front of a hundred TV cameras, and we could have written our own ticket. Every public official with any kind of clout would have weighed in on our side."

"You son of a bitch!" Ben's voice cracked. The weight of the day, the sky, Sam's arrogance choked him. "The farms are backing off. The EPA's all over them. They're paying for the clean-up! And you pull something like *this*? To get *more*?"

"Sometimes you have to hurt what you love in order to save it, Ben. This started as a real marsh fire." Sam nodded toward the armory, in the darkness to the left. "They offered to burn backfires for us to test their new gunk. A simple favor. After that... they were burning cord grass any-way. It was a chance to give the bad guys the black eye they've had coming for years."

"So you destroyed what you spent years protecting?"

"Cord grass'll grow back, Ben. In a year you won't know it was burned. You know that. We didn't ask to be put in this position, but here we are. With an opportunity to do some good, make things better. It'd be irresponsible not to."

"Bailey may die. Will that make things better?"

"Bailey never could stay out of harm's way. You know that, Ben. You notice no one else..."

"When this gets out... " Sam wouldn't sidetrack him this time. His fist was tight, weightless on the door handle beside him.

"Oh, but it won't get out, son. You're idealistic, but you're not stupid. Why repeat that sad family history of yours when you can rewrite it? Help this place like your dad never could.

"This is war, Ben. Make no mistake. We've got to use everything we have. Wild spaces are disappearing faster than we can save them. And not just here. They're drilling in wildlife preserves. They're running Ski-Doos in the Boundary Waters and Yellowstone. Yosemite's so torn up they're locking people out."

"This isn't Yosemite! When people find out *you* OK'd this, there won't be a park here!" He forced his fist back down. "There's no way you can rationalize this! Or blame me."

"This isn't about blame. It's about who has the power to save this and every other wilderness area in the country!" Sam's voice rose as he spoke. Then quieter, "We have to make people care again. That's where you and I come in, son. Loraxes in hobnail boots. We're the only protectors this place has. And we don't have the luxury of letting things work themselves out. We have different responsibilities, different rules."

"Rules are rules, Sam. And there's no way you can keep this secret."

"Oh, stories'll get out. Standard conspiracy theory stuff. But no proof. Your little romp through my office didn't turn up anything, did it?"

"It wasn't me. But it should have been."

Archer hesitated, looking puzzled. Then he recovered.

"Ben, you run your mouth now, there'll be no Park left. Just one continuous subdivision from the river to the Gulf inside two years. Or golf courses. That what you want – 'Cocaine Links' revisited? Finish off what your dad started?"

"This is worse than he ever was!" The car's interior reddened. Ben clutched the door handle and seat to keep his hands down.

Sam slapped Ben's leg. "Remember those Grecian Formula-types hanging out in town? The ones trying to look woodsy in the creased khakis and shiny Banana Republic vests? Gordian Properties folks. They're *real* interested in what kind of protection this place has. Damnedest thing, Gordian's got 2,000 acres just upstream of the park, and plans for condos and 90 holes of golf. And then there's the citrus boys all up and down the river. And the sugar companies. And the offshore drillers."

Ben looked away, over the glowing marsh. Archer believed what he was saying. He made sense. He sounded reasonable. Archer's fingers drummed on the steering wheel, beating out the rhythm of unheard music.

"Ben, what's done is done." The voice was calmer now, rising and falling like a chant, or the beginning of a hymn. "We can't change what happened. But we can fix things, make them better."

"Have you seen the burns? You have *any* idea what thousands of burned acres looks like?"

"Burning so much was a mistake. I admit that, Ben. But we need to move on. We have a chance to restore this place to the way it was 200 years go. You want to be part of that? Or would you rather be the Boy Scout who killed the wilderness with a word?"

"You can't twist things like that, Sam. This... all of it... it's *wrong*!"

"Son, you've got a fine moral sense. That's good. But don't let the pretty sunset blind you to the moccasins. You go public with this, they'll crucify you. You and your conscience, both. They'll impale you on a spike where you can watch the bulldozers work. And after the vultures peck out your eyes, you can listen to 'em haul in fill dirt. But you'll know you did the right thing. You bet. Your conscience handle that?"

The western sky had darkened to a deep red, streaked with black. Darkness swallowed the salt marsh, the road, the car. Sam's scheme went against everything Ben believed, everything Sam had ever inspired in him. But Sam was right about what would happen if the full story got out. *When* it got out, Ben corrected himself. The Hermosa County he knew would disappear forever. The Park Service destroying a wilderness area for political gain would mean a public backlash that would kill the Park and the community that relied on it.

But Sam was also right that the fires couldn't be undone. Ben had to work with what pieces were left. He could fix as much as he could. He'd lose his job, at the very least. He wondered who would look after the backcountry when he was gone. Would they care about the land like he did, or would it be some political appointee from the capitol?

"Ben, I'm out of here in a year. Tops." Sam's voice pulled him back to the car. "After this, with all the attention you've drawn, the job's yours. You'll be me."

"No."

"You'll have free-rein to protect this place the way you want. The way it should be. Go public, you'll never get the chance," Sam said. "You think the good townfolk'll let you walk away? Let you spend the rest of your life lazing out by Walden Pond? You'll be just another Gates who screwed them over. You won't last a day.

"And assuming you get out of here alive, there'll still be a big, impersonal, pissed-off bureaucracy looking to get even. You get funding cut and all kinds of people fired, someone'll get even. If you're lucky, they'll send you to jail."

"I'll deal with that as it comes."

"They'll bury you, Ben. Ship you so far away only a .308 round'll find you."

In the sky, only hints of purple remained, low above the horizon. The dashboard lights reflected green on the window glass. Ben moved his head forward to block it out. He wished he could block out Sam's voice as easily.

"I'm just laying out what'll happen, son. *After* they manufacture the evidence to show you've been a malcontent, borderline postal, and under psychiatric care for years. Maybe even depressed enough to kill yourself." He backhanded Ben's thigh again, making sure Ben was listening. "You got good instincts, Ben. A fine sense of honor. But this is the real world. You got to use that honor wisely."

"I won't lie for you."

"Exactly. A liar for personal gain is just that – a liar. But a liar with the greater good at heart, that's a leader. Your dad learned the difference the hard way. We tell them our side often enough, loud enough, they'll believe us enough for us to do some good. This is *your* chance, Ben. Your duty."

Sam was right. Ben could do the right thing, yet cause more damage than James Gates ever had. Or he could go along with Sam and maybe make up for his dad's mistakes. Was it that clear-cut? It couldn't be. But it sounded so r easonable the way Sam explained it. So easy. Yet neither option felt right. Ben sat still in the darkness, clutching the compass in his shirt pocket. Archer left him in silence the rest of the way into town.

The tourist traps and Indian River citrus stands at the U.S. 41 intersection were a brief blur of floodlight glare, of pink-and-blue neon in the blackness, snapping Ben's thoughts into focus. He had stopped the fires. Ben clung to that. The town, the park, the fire crews were safe now. Wasn't that enough? He should be able to walk away. More lights flashed by, sporadic, then constant as they entered town. The city park was a dark and welcome void. Then Sam turned left, and Park headquarters was in front of them.

Vans and semi-trucks sprouing satellite dishes crammed the parking lot. Racks of photofloods lit the end of the deck nearest the boat ramp in blue-white glare. Time for the live feeds on the evening newscasts. A cluster of reporters and Parks people crowded the deck out front.

"Press'll want to talk to you." Sam's voice echoed from far away. He cut the headlights as they turned into the curving asphalt drive. "You're the ranger's ranger, the man who single-handedly saved Cypress City from ruin. If you want to be..."

Ben sat still, grinding his teeth. He was hesitating. Again. No matter how hard he tried, it always came back to this. He had to do something. A figure broke loose from the crowd, walked toward them.

"Whatcha gonna tell 'em, son?" The voice hung soft in his ear. Archer killed the engine. "Those lights can save you, or they can destroy everything you love."

Across the lawn Ben recognized the silhouette's flowing stride, the sway of her ponytail. He slipped out the car and walked away, angling toward the dark end of the headquarters building and his office. Steps quickened behind him, then he felt a hand on his shoulder.

"Hey! Sammy brought you home? Does that mean good news or bad?"

"Not now, Kel."

"Did you find your pilot? Ben, did you... Hey!"

"The fires are out." He kept walking. If he could get up the side steps, across the far end of the deck and to his office, he could lock the door, sort things out before he had to face anyone.

"Ben! That's wonderful! You've got to tell everyone!"

"I need to... I need space."

Kelly stepped in front of him, hands on his shoulders

and walked backwards matching his stride. "Ben? What happened?"

"Later. Please."

"Uh uh. You fly off with fire in your eyes, Sammy drives you back, and suddenly you're all cryptic? What did you do?"

Ben lifted Kelly's hands from his shoulders. "I don't know. Yet." He stepped around her, then stopped. "Kel, I'm sorry. I just... I'll talk to you when I finish up." He walked up the ramp. Kelly's footsteps followed.

A reporter, *St. Pete Times* maybe, walked out of the snack bar with a Coke in one hand and a chili dog in the other as Ben reached the steps.

"Mr. Gates, any word on the fires?"

"Sam Archer's by the boat ramp."

"They're out!" Kelly yelled from behind him.

The reporter glanced from his food, to the lawn, and back to his food, as if the drink and hot dog were burning his hands. He dropped his food and pulled a notepad from his back pocket. "When? How?"

Ben's stomach rolled. Kelly stepped beside him, intent. He forced a smile. "We're still sorting out the details, probably have a press release later tonight. Tomorrow morning, latest."

"Anything you can give me now?"

Ben imagined the man running down the dock, yelling the news to the other reporters. Sam was right. They had to minimize damage. The fires were out. That was all that mattered. And for now, the only thing he could control was which details got out. By talking privately to *one* reporter.

"Come here." Ben stepped to a picnic table in the building's shadow. "I'll give you what I can, just stay low-key. We... have the fire contained in a small area by Tophet's Mound, hell-and-gone from the town. Nowhere for it to burn but in on itself." The words flowed, another press briefing.

Several people walked past, one carrying a television camera. The cameraman turned toward Ben's voice, squinted into the shadows. "Ben Gates? Fires out?" The others turned and crowded close. The man switched on the camera's floodlight and raised the camera to his shoulder. A woman held a microphone toward Ben.

"Mr. Gates, could you tell us the current status of the fires?"

Ben tried to keep smiling, shrugged at the *Times* reporter. To the side, Kelly stood watching him. He was still hesitating. No. He had already acted. He would do his job. His duty. What was necessary. Anything else was posturing.

"The fires are contained and pose no threat to the town. We should finish them off in the morning."

"Any truth to rumors the fires were deliberately set?" The television reporter pushed the microphone closer. Kelly's eyes were locked on his, her eyebrows raised.

"No." His voice could have come from the air, from the ground itself. "No, we've found nothing like that." He looked away from Kelly, toward the darkened parking lot. There, faint behind the glare of the television flood lights, Sam Archer stood, smiling, nodding.

## 12

"Kelly was already seeing Henry when Ben came back from college, you know," Amanda Morehouse said, "and eyeball-deep in Mangrove Underground plotting, though she got off scot-free later. And Ben, poor thing, was none the wiser. She always did have him by the nose, and Ben always blind to that. Anything bad that ever happened to him started with Kelly Barnes. He could have done so much better.

"So that night they're sitting at one of the tables by the river, little candle-lanterns flickering between them, and dock lights all yellowy on the water," Amanda said, "with Ben looking out across the river while Kelly chattered on about work or whatever. Like she ever cared about anything except getting attention. And poor Ben, fresh in town, as unseeing as ever.

"Anyway, they're at the table behind us and talking loud – you couldn't help but overhear – she's babbling and Ben's staring into the dark, not saying anything. I guess she finally noticed, because she stopped, then goes, 'Penny for 'em.'

"And Ben goes, 'You changed.' He saw a glimmer of truth – I knew him well enough to hear that in his voice.

"Kelly didn't. She stalled, wondering what he meant, what he knew. Then she's like, 'No, not really,' all soft-like.

"Ben shook his head. 'At the show today... I didn't know you.'"

"'We've been apart. I'm just glad you're back early!' She tried to sound excited, but you could hear the lie. If you knew her like I did, anyway. One person's 'charm' is another person's 'two-faced.' It always amazed me I was the only one could see it.

"And Ben's like, 'You could have been killed.'

"'Ben! I've never felt so alive!' She leaned in close then, turning it on. 'In two minutes with Rap-Tor I turned that carnival sideshow into something real, something... spiritual. You had to have felt that!' She talked like that, Kelly. Still does. DeWayne was so right to cut her loose.

"'You almost turned it into a feeding frenzy.'

"'Oh, he was fine. I wouldn't have jumped in if he weren't. I'm not stupid.'

I choked on a bit of salad at that. Kelly glared. She always was hateful to me – I have no idea why. Then she turned back to Ben. 'And anyway, it won't happen again – I got fired, remember?'

"'And you're OK with that?'

"'Earth to Ben?' she goes, all condescending. 'That's what I've been talking about? Forestry needs firefighters.'

"And Ben's like, 'That's better?' You could see he was hurting – he cared about her, and her giving nothing back.

*I wanted to walk over and hug him. And smack her – lay her out like Ben did with that dodgeball her first day at school.*

*But it was their date and none of my business. I kept my back to them and went on with my supper.*

*"'I've been doing it volunteer,' she goes, 'so it's not that big of a jump. And the pay's way better.'*

*"And Ben goes, 'What about your spirituality?' I had to smile at that. He was blind to her, but not dumb.*

*"'This'll put me in the real world, doing real work, honest work – not just scamming tourists and telling myself I'm somehow educating them. The show could be so much more, but it never will be.'*

*She reached over and grabbed his hands, she was so caught up in herself. 'Sometimes you just have to make a jump – have faith in yourself and the world and just jump. You know what I mean?'*

*"'No. I think...'*

*"'Exactly,' she cut him off. 'You think too much. Sometimes you have to do what feels right, even if it seems crazy. Get your hands dirty. You, we've both been... just being, not doing.'*

*"Ben looked away. I could tell it was starting to click just how crazy Kelly was. And how wrong they were for each other. I mean, how could it not click, with her rambling on about nothing but herself? From a table away I could tell it wasn't a happy reunion. Far from it. 'We're OK, right?' he finally said.*

*"'Oh, of course, silly. Why?' I wanted to get up and slap her then, but it wasn't my place. I figured I'd talk to*

*Ben later, privately, for his own good. And I've regretted not ever since.*

*"'Things feel... different,' he said.*

*"'We've been apart,' Kelly goes, 'that's all, seeing other people and all.'*

*"Ben just stared at her. There was surprise and hurt in his eyes, plain as anything. Kelly went all still and quiet, too. Finally.*

*"'That doesn't mean I don't love you,' she said at last. She slid a hand over his, squeezed.*

*"Ben still didn't move. After a minute he goes, 'We're great together.' He said it so quiet I had to strain to hear.*

*"'We are, aren't we?' The corners of her eyes crinkled as she turned the charm up another notch. 'The only thing wrong is that fairy-tale image of us in your head. Set that aside. Accept what we have.' She squeezed his hand again and goes, 'We may not be perfect, but we're pretty phenomenal. We just need to figure out where we go with that.'*

*"She looked up in the air then. Ben and I did, too, following her gaze. A pinpoint of light streaked across the sky and reflected in the water. Then another. And another. All over the courtyard people looked up at the stars shooting across the sky.*

*"'Oooh!!' Kelly goes. 'The Perseids! I forgot!' Like she knew. Like she had scheduled it or something. She stood up, as if that would give her a better view. All it did was block mine.*

*"What little breeze there was swished her hair across her face. With her eyes off him and her face covered, it was*

like Ben came out from under her spell for a moment.

"Kelly missed that. She was like, 'This is so cool!' She pulled her hair back and glanced down at him. 'You're back early, and now the stars are...'

"Ben stood up, leaned across the table and kissed her. It surprised me as much as it did her.

"He says, 'We've been apart too much. I missed you.'

"And Kelly goes, 'Yeah. A letter a day was my first clue.'

"Ben studied her for a couple of breaths, then goes, 'Nothing would be better than spending the rest of my life with you.' My heart just sunk for him at that.

"Kelly smiled, looking all innocent, and goes, 'You said that before. So did I.' I choked again, nearly spitting baked grouper across the table, just knowing she came up with it first.

"'It's just... scary, is all,' he said.

"'Scary?' she said.

"'To let you down... to not measure up.'

"And she comes back with, 'You could never do that.' It was enough to make you sick.

They stood there grinning at each other, in front of God and everyone, for about forever. Then, out of nowhere, Ben pulls out a ring and holds it out to her.

"'We can do it whenever you want, but this is for now.'

"Kelly, she just stared, playing it up like she was surprised, then goes, 'Oh, Ben, yes! Yes!' She lunged for him then, almost knocked over the table, and hugged him so tight I thought she'd kill him.

"Ben worked free and pulled back, holding her hands. 'Lets get out of here,' he said real low and even, not wanting to make a scene. Like it mattered – everyone was looking at them by then, some even being so silly as to clap. Kelly smiled, then leaned close and kissed him again.

"They walked hand-in-hand up the pier. I had to go to the ladies' room, and ended up walking behind them. He slipped an arm around her waist and she leaned into him, eating it up. The damn crickets and tree frogs made it hard to hear.

"Ben whispered something and Kelly laughed. 'Be happy, Ben,' she goes. 'Is that so hard?'

"'It's more complicated than that. We're OK, though?'

"'If you let us be.'

"He kissed her then, and brushed the hair from her face. It was enough to make you sick, him carrying on that way.

"Then he goes, 'I love you, Kel.' Just like that. 'I have no idea what either of us will end up doing. But if we're together, it has to be great.'

"Kelly's eyes sparkled with the pathway lights. She knew she had him.

"'You and that ideal world of yours,' she goes. 'You're pretty cool, you know that?' She closed her eyes and kissed him again, playing it to the hilt. Ben cupped her face in his hands, and I had to walk away.

There was no way he would ever see fires, Henry Moton, or a future without Kelly. Though he'd have been better off if he had. We all would have.

13
—

Ben locked the office door behind him and collapsed on the couch, quiet at last in the cool air and dim light filtering through the blinded window. He had spent the night and much of the morning scrambling from interviews to press releases, keeping busy, shying away from the implications of his decision. Now, with the reporters at lunch, he was finally alone. Kelly was still out with the fire crews. He hadn't seen Sam since that first briefing the night before. The afternoon press conference was hours away.

He had done what he had to do. His opinion, Kelly's opinion, anyone's opinion no longer mattered. Opinions were luxuries. And Sam was right: Ben had no physical proof to show anyone other than some blurry cell phone photos. If he went public, it would be his word against Sam's and the US Army. He closed his eyes and let the reporters, Sam, Kelly, and the oily feeling in his gut fall away.

The dreams came quickly: firefighters in red Mangrove Underground jackets reaching up to him, eyes pleading; flames arching over his head as he tried to run, his legs mired in wet ash; Sam Archer's eyes bright in the darkness; he and

Bailey soaring above the fires, choking on napalm fumes, unable to speak above the beat of a helicopter's rotors. Their insistent '*wump-wump-wump*' beat louder, more solid.

Ben felt the couch beneath him, opened his eyes. Someone beating on something. Kelly's voice, threatening to kick her way in. He rose, cracked the door. Kelly shoved past him in a reek of wood smoke, still wearing her boots and asbestos pants.

"I don't know whether to slap you or kiss you!" She glanced from the desk to the jumbled couch cushions to his rumpled shirt. "Sleeping? With the two-way off?"

"Fires out?" Ben rubbed his eyes, the dreams still fresh.

"Out? Ben, another house burned today!" Her voice shook.

"No. The fires are out." He was still dreaming. Or had the Colonel lied? He closed the door and relocked it.

"We put them out. For good. But before we could, the Wilson place..."

Ben felt for the desk beside him, knew it supported him though he couldn't feel it. All this should have been over. No one was supposed to be hurt.

"DeWayne wouldn't leave," Kelly said. "Amanda Morehouse went back. By the time we got there..." She took a deep breath, then another, her jaw muscles clenching. "We couldn't..."

"Who?"

"Both of them."

"Kel, you... we... did everything we could." He watched Kelly, but he spoke to himself, cold and numb. He had to be still dreaming. Old Wilson and Amanda weren't gone. The fires were out. He had stopped them.

Kelly stepped close and wrapped her arms around him, shaking. Her cheek felt moist on his neck, her hands warm on his back. Ben held her, too tight, not sure if he was comforting Kelly or himself as he stroked her hair. She shouldn't hurt. He should take the hurt away.

"It's OK. It's not your fault." He could have been reciting the alphabet. He had done this, caused the pain that poured from her, lanced through him and filled the room. He *should* have seen what Sam was doing, acted sooner, stopped things before yesterday, before...

Kelly pulled away. "Sorry. I couldn't do that in front of people."

He wanted to hold her again, but he was too numb. He felt closer to Kelly now than he had ever thought to be again. He had his best friend back. He wouldn't lose her this time. He clung to that, needing the connection, the approval. She trusted him, as she trusted no one else. She deserved to know everything. But how could he tell her? He hated himself. He couldn't bear to have Kelly hate him, too.

"Ben? What? I know about the fax."

"Fax?"

"Your 'anonymous' one." She glanced past him, to the computer and fax machine. "Every paper and channel got it. The Park let the Army burn the backcountry? I'm so proud! You stopped the fires last night, then you exposed Sammy this morning. He'll have hell to pay, and he deserves it!"

"I didn't send a fax." His voice echoed from far away, from someplace cold and isolated. How had word gotten out? And so quickly? He stepped away from Kelly. Had Sam set him up? No, Ben knew too much for that. Who, then? No one from the Army. One environmentally-conscious GI could have sent a fax, but Ben remembered Colonel Smith's face. The colonel would have all his men billeted far from contact with the outside world for a while. He fumbled for the couch. Kelly was talking again.

"This is what had you so upset last night, isn't it?" Kelly sat next to him, her knee warm against his thigh.

He had to tell her, but the words wouldn't come. "It's...complicated," he whispered. Ben rocked forward, studying specks on the linoleum floor. He had thought his decision the night before would bring him peace. It wasn't perfect, but he had done what caused the most good. Or the least harm. The complications were supposed to have died with the fires.

Instead, Miss Adele... Amanda... The fate of the Park, the town, faded in comparison with those deaths. Sam couldn't shrug them off as a 'wild conspiracy theory.' Neither could Ben.

He imagined himself at the afternoon press conference, one of Sam's prepared releases in-hand, denying any involvement with the fires. Then he imagined questions about the Wilson and Amanda, denying any responsibility. The office felt colder. Omitting facts, telling half-truths about burned grass was one thing. But people, family friends even, had died because of Sam Archer's ambition. Denying accountability for that... Specks in the linoleum became cameras, faces, floodlights... he couldn't do it.

He blinked, changed the scene, imagined himself shouting everything he knew into the microphones. No. He couldn't do that, either. They would blame him, the community. He would be just another Gates who betrayed them. He wouldn't repeat his father's mistake. But what choice did he have? Ben glanced at the window. Running away would solve nothing. The walls leaned closer. He couldn't change what happened, but how could he make things better?

"Ben? Talk to me." Kelly's hand settled softly on his arm. "I want to help, but I can't if you won't let me."

His lips tingled, as if the air had been sucked from the room. How could he tell her? Ben tried to swallow, gagged, fighting for air, his arms tight across his ribs. He was safe here in the darkened office. Until the press conference. Fear came then, rising like water in the sloughs after a storm, unstoppable, overflowing of its own accord. He needed help.

"It's my fault," he heard himself say. "Amanda..." His stomach tightened. "My fault, not yours."

"You did great."

"Not soon enough. Not... enough."

Ben hesitated. To Kelly the issue would be simple, easy. But 'simple' and 'easy' wouldn't work. Not now. It had to be right. His throat was too tight. He forced the words out.

"Sam OK'd it. All of it. We got free back burns, they got to test some new napalm-stuff." Someone else could have been speaking through him, using his voice to form the words. "For PR. We would save the town, look like heroes, expand the Park, double our budget."

Kelly could have been a statue beside him. He didn't dare look at her. "Anyone found out, we were screwed." He closed his eyes, pressed his thumbs against his temples. "I found out."

"And you stopped it."

He wanted to say 'yes,' simplify it all, justify his actions, but he couldn't. Not to Kelly. Not with her blaming herself for the deaths. Ben shook his head. "Sam called it off. At the armory. I knew that when the reporters cornered me. I just... didn't tell them."

"Ben! Why?"

"If people find out the Park Superintendent torched the Park for political gain, they'll gut the Park. The Park goes under, the town goes under." Yet something inside screamed that even if he had told the truth last night, the Morehouse place would still have burned. His actions had nothing to do with those deaths. He clung to that. They weren't his fault.

"That's Sammy talking," Kelly said. "And those deaths are on his hands. Don't put your head in that noose."

"Right and wrong aren't always so clear-cut, Kel..." his voice trailed off. It had made sense last night, but not so much now. "This was supposed to help everyone. No one could have found out. Only me, Sam, and an army colonel knew."

"And you didn't send the fax?"

Ben shook his head.

"And the colonel..."

He shook his head again.

"Oh, Ben" She slipped an arm around his shoulders. "He hung you out to dry. Just like your... everyone."

Ben clamped his eyes tight. He stood beside the burning barge again, saw himself standing still, Henry holding James Gates, the disgust in Kelly's eyes, all lit dull orange by the flames. He saw his mother, still and pale at the backcountry campsite, himself rummaging through the med kit. He was as useless now as he had ever been.

"No," he whispered. "This hurts Sam more than it does me."

'Not if he can pin everything on you, step in as the rescuer." Kelly's voice came as soft as his own. "He's like that."

"He's better off if ... oh, God, I was stupid, wasn't I?"

"Ben, when have you ever done the smart thing? Seriously. You do stupid things. But always for the best reasons. That's why I love you."

Ben froze, transfixed by the words. Fires, conspiracies, deaths disappeared as the words sank in.

"Oh... that's not what I meant... I mean, I did, but... you know what I mean. Not like that." Her arm slid across his shoulders again. "Ben, you made a small mistake last night. Damned public, but small. Not turning Sammy in now, not telling the authorities everything, that's a big mistake. They call those 'felonies.'"

He barely heard her over his heartbeat. It was happening again – every time he had ever acted on his convictions, people had been hurt. Or died. Every time he trusted himself, asserted himself, that sense of self evaporated like swamp fog at dawn. Kelly, Sam, even Henry in his time, they knew who they were and could act on that. Ben, and his choices, always went wrong.

"Ben? Listen to me." Kelly knelt in front of him, hands on his arms. "Ever since we were little I've looked up to you. Yeah, you screw up. A lot. But I've never seen you stray from what you believe. That makes... you make me a better person. There's no one else I can say that about." She squeezed his arms so hard they hurt. "No matter how bad things got between us, I've always respected you."

"Don't." He couldn't look at her, at the brown eyes staring at him so intently . "I ... just want something to turn out right. Once. I want to... fix... untangle... make things perfect again."

"You can't, Ben." Kelly pulled his head up so her eyes were inches from his own.

"I can," he said. "It's there. Always. Waiting for me to want it enough." The room blurred. His face felt hot, wet.

He looked down, closed his eyes, tried to block out her face, the smell of her hair, her breath. He wanted to hold her, curl up in her arms, but he couldn't. Not anymore. "All I ever wanted was to make you proud."

"So turn him in."

The floor tilted. He needed her respect more than anything else. But he couldn't even look at her. The Ben she cared about, the Ben he wanted to be, didn't exist, couldn't exist in a real world filled with real people and real problems. Wanting and willing could no longer keep that illusion spinning three-dimensionally in the air around him. He shied back into himself, to find... nothing. He teetered between that inner emptiness and the chaos around him, afraid to breathe or think or make any move that might upset that balance. He needed to stand. Act. But he was tired. So tired. If he could sit here, still and quiet, for a moment, for a while, the darkness would recede and he could rest. Or maybe the darkness would swallow him after all.

"Ben?" Kelly's voice came faint, shaking, from somewhere nearby. "DeWayne and Amanda are dead because of Sam. He'll be blaming you."

"He can't, wouldn't," Ben said. But the room seemed to empty of air again as he spoke. That was exactly Sam's style. But only with his enemies. He and Ben were on the same side. Sam had gone out of his way to help Ben, to promote him. "I owe him."

"Don't, Ben. The park will survive this. And Sam. The town, too. Will you?"

She was right. Amanda and Miss Adele outweighed any debt he owed Sam Archer. His father's voice echoed in his head, as clearly as if James Gates were standing beside him. 'It's not the thing you do, Ben, it's how you do a thing.' But how could he turn on Sam so quickly? Of course, James Gates hadn't followed his own advice. Not when it counted, anyway. But that didn't make that advice any less valid.

"OK, Ben, how about this: what if Sammy didn't send the fax, but thinks you did? What do you think his next move will be?"

"I have to talk to Sam," he said. "Ask him point-blank. If I can find him before anyone finds me."

"And if he's already burned you?"

"Then I roll over on him. But I have to talk to him first."

Ben choked again, straining for air. Every point was valid, but put together none of it made sense. He was right. But so was Kelly. The arguments coiled back on themselves, started over at a more fevered pitch. He needed time and space to think. But the press conference was in two hours.

"We'll figure this out together, OK, Ben?" He felt her hands slide over his, shake them gently. "It's crazy to face Sammy now, in this situation, without a backup plan, right? How about this – write it all out, everything that happened, everything you and Sam said. We'll make copies. E-mail them to ourselves to date and time-stamp them. I can notarize a hard copy, mail it to my dad. That'll give you a day or so to sort things out, And some legal protection if things go wrong."

Kelly's familiar scent of jasmine, her once-familiar warmth surrounded him. He didn't feel like writing anything, or even moving from the couch. He wanted to curl up in her scent and hide forever.

"No time. The briefing."

"Forget the press conference, Ben. Let Sammy handle it." Kelly pulled him to his feet and walked him to the desk.

"I can't type," he whispered. "I can't see."

"Then talk. I'll type." She slid into his chair and guided Ben to the edge of the desk. "Now, when did you first hear of the fires?"

Ben saw nothing but the pale green linoleum between his feet. He whispered, to himself, to the darkness, everything that had happened in the past few days: his talks with Sam, Kelly's reports, his day on the fire line and all the details that hadn't made sense, it all flowed from him, unstoppable. He spared nothing, and no one, himself least of all. As he spoke he felt lighter, cleansed, as if ridding himself of all the doubt, the self-recrimination of the past days. He felt his voice grow stronger, though he still spoke in a whisper.

Kelly typed without interrupting. When Ben finished, she laid a hand on his arm. "You're a knife at his throat, Ben. You know that? He can't let you run loose knowing all this."

Ben's desk phone rang, startling them both. Ben shook his head 'no.' Kelly motioned him to be quiet, then picked up the receiver.

"Parks, Kelly Barnes... Haven't seen him... Either of them... Oh, God." Her voice broke. "OK, tell them press release by 3:30." She hung up and turned to Ben.

"Bailey just died. And Sammy's AWOL. He left this all on you, Ben." She glanced to the door, then around the room, her gaze lingering on the window blinds. "I'll call my dad. He'll have the best lawyer in the county here in 10 minutes."

"I'm going to find him." His voice was faint, but he saw what he had to do, clearer than anything Kelly could suggest. Reciting the past days' events, and now Bailey's death, had pulled everything into focus. He would do what was right. He would do things properly this time. He felt power, confidence flowing through him again. "I'll bring him back to answer for everything, even if I go down, too."

"Find him where? That's crazy."

"Half-dozen places near town. If I can keep out of sight. But he's probably headed for the sticks. The old Still-water camp, probably. Says he thinks better out there."
Kelly shook her head. "It'll look like you're running away. That plays right into Sammy's hands."

"Then I have to catch him before they catch me."

"Your conscience is gonna get you hurt, you know that?" Kelly studied him, arms crossed. "You'll want to slip out that window. Now." She hugged him quick. "I'll send this, mail copies, then call Dad. No – you need as big a safety net as you can get."

"If I don't find Sam in town this evening, I'll need a place to hole up."

Kelly smiled. "I'll be home by six."

14

# FORMER COMMISSIONER'S LIFE, DEATH POLARIZE TOWN

*By Wayne Ebanks*
State Staff Writer

*CYPRESS CITY, Fla. – The discovery of a former Hermosa County Commissioner's body, nearly a month after he failed to appear for sentencing on bribery, grand theft and racketeering charges, has further divided this small coastal community of fishermen and retirees.*

*James Gates, who served one term on the county's zoning board and two terms on the county commission, was one of the 'Gates Eight,' local officials and business people convicted of exchanging votes for money, buying narcotics with that money, and spending the proceeds on large tracts of land bordering the Catahoula River and along the coast southward.*

*Gates' body was found Thursday evening at the wheel of his car, closed in a Cypress City self-storage unit, the apparent victim of carbon monoxide poisoning.*

*Hermosa County Sheriff's Office officials say the car's ignition switch was on and its gas tank empty.*

*Autopsy results are expected next week, though authorities say they do not suspect foul play.*

*That has not kept some in Hermosa County from doubting Gates' death was suicide.*

*At the heart of the controversy is what Gates and the others planned for the waterfront tracts. Both sides acknowledge court records showing the land slated for a 72-hole golf resort, but they differ widely in explaining James Gates' motivation.*

*News of the discovery was the main topic of discussion at Maisie's Skillet, a downtown breakfast nook frequented by Cypress City's natives.*

*"James stood tall, made us proud of him" said Skillet owner Frank Marish, a fourth-generation Cypress City shrimper who grew up with Gates. "He did wrong, or was forced to, but he was a good man, with Hermosa's interests at heart."*

*Across the square at the government complex, Gates' fellow commissioner Diane Cowper isn't so sure. "James Gates abused the public trust for personal gain, was caught and publicly tried," she said. "For someone who saw himself as a man of the people, that had to have been unbearable."*

## "A Local Hero"

*James Gates' meteoric rise from backwater fisherman to one of the most powerful politicians in Hermosa County is the stuff of local legend. Born into an old-time Cypress City family previously noted for Prohibition-era rum-running, James Gates carried on in his father's, and grandfather's legal practice of commercial fishing, supplying fish, shrimp and crabs to area restaurants.*

*That way of life changed for Gates and many other locals during the latter part of the decade. Retirees and second-home owners discovered Hermosa County. Seemingly overnight Cypress City was transformed from a town of working class beer-drinkers to one of more leisurely wine-sippers.*

*As the population went upscale, so did property values. Soon many natives complained it was too difficult to make a living in what was once a backwoods fishing village. "The crab trap ban's what brought it to a head," said Maisie's regular DeWayne Wilson. "Locals were already unhappy with the transplants flooding in, making it tough for a working family to survive where they'd lived for four, five generations."*

*Lobbied by new, relatively moneyed residents, the Hermosa County Commission banned the storage of crab traps, fish nets, or commercial fishing boats within sight of public roads in communities newly-zoned residential.*

*One of the first and most vocal opponents of the measure was James Gates. In defiance of the new ordinance,*

*Gates immediately moved several dozen crab traps from under his stilt house to the roadside edge of his property, then draped fishing nets over the lot.*

*"He drew a good bit of fire for that," Wilson said. "But next thing you knew, we all had our traps and nets out in plain view. Showing we still had some fight left. County couldn't make all of us pay, or arrest us, and we counted that a victory."*

*James Gates, still grieving over the death of his wife on a backcountry camping trip, seemed to find solace in a righteous cause. Never involved in local politics before, Gates began attending commission meetings and zoning hearings, taking every opportunity to expound the local viewpoint.*

*"He used it to distract him from losing Beth," said Sharky's Bar owner Joe Douglas. "He was hitting back as best he knew how, knowing he'd lose, but still fighting the good fight. I think they put him on the zoning board to just shut him up – better to have the mule inside the tent pissing out than outside pissing in.*

*"They just had no idea how much that particular mule could piss."*

*To the surprise of many, James Gates proved a natural politician. Though he spoke sparingly during board meetings, he was busy behind the scenes cultivating allies, building coalitions and currying favors.*

*"Folks knew if they had a problem, they could go to Mr. Gates, and he'd make things right," said Amanda More-*

*house, sipping coffee. "After being beat-down so long, he was our ray of hope."*

*By the end of the year, Gates had a line item on the ballot, a public vote, and the trap ban was repealed.*

## "Crossing The Line"

*With a grassroots groundswell behind him, James Gates was voted county commissioner at the next election. By that time opponents realized they had underestimated him. They focused on negating his influence on the commission.*

*"He said the right things, and he sounded good, until you analyzed what he was really saying," said Cowper, a longtime commissioner and James Gates adversary. "He claimed to want the best for the county, for its people, but what he really wanted was for everything to go back 20, 30, 40 years."*

*If Gates' populist message resonated with old-time Hermosa residents, it rang harsh with the newcomers who were quickly becoming the county's majority.*

*"Progress, by definition, is moving forward," local Veterans of Foreign Wars commander Peter Martinelli said. "James Gates never understood that. And that was his undoing."*

*As compromise solutions became harder to achieve, James Gates turned to more creative means. He began working quietly with members of the business community – bankers, builders, citrus growers – giving in on larger issues dear to his constituency in exchange for smaller favors.*

*The first sign of trouble came early in Gates' second term, when a zoning change appeared last-minute on a commission agenda. The proposed changes ceded several agricultural combines unprecedented right-of-way to swamp land upstream of the nearby Wilderness Park.*

*James Gates spoke eloquently against the proposal, delaying the vote until late that night and eliminating any opportunity for public discussion.*

*Commissioners Hector Ramirez and Alice McKinney, both Hermosa County natives, voted for the measure. So did James Gates.*

*"I was stunned," Cowper said. "It was a complete 180 on everything he – and they – had come to represent."*

*Spurred by public complaint, the state attorney's office began an investigation of the agriculture companies' activities in Hermosa County and their connections with James Gates.*

*Two years later, conspiracy and racketeering charges were filed against commissioners Gates, Ramirez and McKinney, as well as local real estate agents Joe Peddiway and Lonnie Jenkins, property office clerk LeAnn Kile, longtime Gates enemy Delmore Moton, and Flor-Agra CEO Gerry Willard.*

## "CRIME AND PUNISHMENT"

*The Gates Eight trial riveted public attention in Hermosa County for months. Prosecutors presented a case of private business buying government influence, highlighted by double-dealing and drug runs gone awry.*

*James Gates had his hands in all of it.*

*"He rationalized his greed as helping the public cause," said Cowper. "Take donations from business and use it to buy up soon-to-be prime real estate before big developers could get it."*

*The problem was, the agriculture payoffs couldn't come close to funding James Gates' dreams. A gambler at heart, Gates figured to parlay the payoff money into a bankroll big enough to save the entire county.*

*With two of the five commissioners backing him, Gates was assured of a majority vote for any issues he wanted ramrodded through the approval process. The Flor-Agra money, combined with what he skimmed from public funds, paid for loads of cocaine, hauled into Cypress City on Delmore Moton's shrimp boat.*

*Armed with money from Moton's drug sales, local real estate agents – and Gates' boyhood friends – Peddiway and Jenkins began buying properties along the Catahoula under assumed names. Gates' sometime-girlfriend LeAnn Kile was quick to reassure anyone who questioned the many lots being sold to buyers named 'Winston,' 'Merit,' 'Benson,' 'Hedges,' and 'Raleigh.'*

*During the trial, the land quickly became known as 'Smoker's Acres,' then 'Cocaine Links.'*

*"James Gates' plan, as described in court, was to buy waterfront property at current value to hold in unofficial*

public trust for those who might need it later," said Judge George Barnes, who tried Gates and the others.

"He was lining his pockets, pure and simple,' said Cowper. "If the golf complex deal had gone through, that would have been the end of the Wilderness Park. He and his cronies could have retired to Rio."

Others don't see it so clear-cut.

"If James Gates said it was for the public good, it was," said Marish. "He may have crossed a line or two, but he was a man of his word."

## "A Family Affair"

Whether for public good or personal gain, the wild scheme might have succeeded if not for James Gates' son. Recently returned from college, Ben Gates stumbled across his father's plans by accident. It was he who tipped off Hermosa County deputies, then led them to a clandestine rendezvous with Delmore Moton's son, Henry, on his own vandalistic rampage, deep in the swamp.

"Henry was the younger generation joining in James' Gates' fight," Frank Marish said. "Stepping in where more drastic action was needed. But Ben Gates was the clod in the churn."

Though the younger Moton was never apprehended, Ben Gates recovered enough of his father's documents to have James Gates and the others convicted on multiple counts of grand theft and racketeering.

James Gates stood defiant at his trial, admitting what he had done, but refusing to call it wrongdoing.

Gates was free on bail, awaiting sentencing, when he vanished. That disappearance spawned a host of Robin Hood-type stories about James Gates.

Then police discovered his body in a storage unit he had once rented. Legends gave way to conspiracy theories. "If Mr. Gates did have plans to sell that land for a golf course, you can bet it wasn't his idea," said Amanda Morehouse.

DeWayne Wilson put it more succinctly, giving voice to many natives' suspicions. "Someone called in a debt, made sure they got the land, then made sure James wasn't able to talk about it.

"Guns blazing, that was James' style – not choking in a car like that."

Ed Fielding, the Hermosa County Sheriff's Office lead detective on the case, thinks otherwise. "James Gates was caught red-handed. When it came time to answer for it, he couldn't face the people who had put so much faith in him. Simple as that."

Diane Cowper echoed those sentiments. "With a depressed economy, a way of life dying, people resort to extremes. The irony was he sold out to the interests he spent so much of his life defying."

The breakfast crowd at Maisie's, though, is still willing to give Gates the benefit of the doubt.

"He meant well, and did good for us," Frank Marish said. "Things just took on a life of their own. Could have been any of us, really, if we were to be honest with ourselves."

## 15

The Catahoula River wound gray and lacquer-smooth in the predawn light. Mangrove roots and downed branches jutted up from the flat water along the shoreline, mirroring black against the gray. Leaves, wisps of fog, white ibises in trees blurred past as Ben skimmed upriver at full throttle. Ben kept the Dusky midstream, watching for snags as he rounded each bend. Ahead were the Canebrake tangles, then Buck's Bay to the northeast. And Sam Archer, running full-stick in his Grady White. Sam was far ahead by now, but there were few side channels before the bay. Ben, with his single engine, couldn't hope to overtake him, but he could track Sam if he followed close enough. Archer wouldn't be going to the 'Brakes – it was too swampy for the Grady, and there was only one narrow channel leading to and from the area. Bucks and the maze of channels south of there were more likely.

Ben had no idea why Sam would be so far from the Stillwater camp. He had seen the Grady White cutting from a side channel in the half-light, then speeding upriver ahead of him. As if the driver was surprised to see another boat. Ben had been just as surprised. It had to be Sam. Trying to hide. Or hiding evidence. If Ben could stay close enough, outthink Sam, he could trap Archer, drag him back and hand him to Judge Barnes.

He rubbed his eyes with one hand. Kelly's jasmine scent clung to his arm, swirled in the windshadow behind the Dusky's console. He had meant to spend the night on her couch, nothing more. But the stress of the past few days had re-awakened old patterns. Comfortable patterns. Ben had left well before sunup. Kelly had smiled when he rolled out of bed, then pulled his pillow close and fell back asleep before he was out of the room. Ben felt the chill inside him ease slightly.

Without Kelly, without her belief in him, without her urging him on, he would have given up. She knew him, better than anyone. Yet she still believed in him. He clung to that as tightly as they had clung to each other the night before. Sleeping beside her again, Ben had dreamed of her, waking repeatedly until dreams and reality blurred and the line between himself and Kelly disappeared. The thought of disappointing her now terrified him more than the emptiness he had felt inside himself the day before.

The sky glowed a pale red behind the mangroves to his right. Ben caught himself humming, then grinned when he realized it was *Good Day, Sunshine*. He rounded the final curve into Buck's Bay and eased the throttle back to idle. The broad water glistened orange and pink with the sunrise. Across the bay the first fingernail curve of the sun slipped above a horizon dark with low mangrove islands. An orange pinprick flickered from the mangroves across the water to his right.  Campers at the Croom Creek ground site starting breakfast.

The Dusky rocked in its own wake for a moment, then settled as the waves rippled past and out into the bay. Wisps of fog drifted through the mangroves to his left, shadowy figures flitting through the trees at water level.  He smiled, remembering his imagined Nunnehi encounter after the fire fight.  He could use supernatural help to find Archer. He knew the swamp, knew how Sam thought, but there was a lot of territory to search. Assuming it was Sam in the boat. A line of wood storks glided overhead.  Ben switched off the engine and closed his eyes.  Kelly and his mom would be proud.  He concentrated, feeling the wind, water, and wildlife flow around him.  He had lost touch with that lately.  He felt himself relax for the first time in days.  If he could reconnect with the rhythms of this place, as he had with Kelly, he could find Sam.  Find himself.

Ben shook his head to clear those thoughts.  He had to focus on the Grady, on Sam.  Personal worries were a luxury now.  He had to think clearly, a step ahead of Sam.  Mosquitoes hummed near his ears.  Frogs creaked in the trees around him. Wavelets lapped against the boat's hull.  An osprey keened somewhere overhead.  The clean, salty smell of the marsh at high tide surrounded him.  A hint of Kelly's perfume.  He saw her on her side sleeping, face cradled on the pillow, hair fanned out behind her and curling across her cheek.  Wood smoke.  He remembered joking with Bailey before that last flight, holding a coughing Bailey when all the world seemed burned.  But this was campfire smoke.  The burns were miles to the north. Twin outboards whined in the distance. He saw himself brush the hair from Kelly's face, saw her eyes open to meet his. The outboards whined louder. He wondered if Kelly were up yet. Probably not. She was never up before 10:00 if she didn't have to work.

A white boat burst into the bay from a channel 300 yards ahead of him. Even from across the bay, Ben recognized the hard lines of a Grady. The boat spun and sped back the way it had come. Ben fumbled for the ignition and slammed the throttle forward. Sam was faster but would have to throttle back in the narrow channels. Why would Sam fly into the bay, then turn and run back so quickly? Had he seen Ben and the Dusky? Doubtful, from so far. He could be blowing off steam. "Proficiency driving," Sam always called it.

Ben raced up the channel where Sam had gone. The foam from the Grady's wake still streaked the water. Ben followed it through creeks and side channels, winding generally east and southeast. Ben hadn't been this direction for years. Many turns were unfamiliar, but he followed the foam trail as quickly as he dared. If the creeks were clear enough for the deeper-drafted Grady, the Dusky should have no trouble. Mangroves crowded closer. Branches brushed the Dusky's sides and blocked Ben's view. He throttled back to make the tighter turns. In the narrower channels the foam dissipated into the maze of tree roots. Twice he had to guess which turn to take. He was losing ground. How would Sam think?

Southeast somewhere was Coot Bay. That would give Archer the best chance to lose anyone following him. From there Sam could go up to the Canebrakes, down the Cheela River to the Gulf, or simply hole up on any of a dozen islets. If Sam was out of sight before Ben reached the bay, Ben would never track him across the open water. He nudged the throttle forward, pushing the skiff as fast as he dared. To his left, cypress tops broke the skyline, tall above the acres of mangroves. Trusting a hunch, Ben steered hard left at the next channel.

The creek narrowed, snaking through the brush. The cypress loomed higher. If he was right, the trees were the cypress head at the western end of Moccasin Creek. From there it was a straight shot into Coot Bay. If he could squeeze the Dusky through the narrow creek, he could get through in time to catch the Grady.

He rounded a bend, and the creek emptied into a small bay. The cypress grove towered to his right. Redfish Bay. Ben smiled, turned the boat downstream, then dog-legged right into Moccasin Creek. He hunched over the console as branches slapped across his head and back. High tide. Plenty of water beneath the prop. But it pushed the open boat into the overhanging branches.

"No snakes. No snakes." Ben shuddered, his eyes half-closed. He knelt beside the console, eyes level with the gunwales, steering with one hand and blocking branches with the other. The plastic steering wheel slid slick in his sweating hand. If there were moccasins in the trees, he would hit them before he saw them. Ben bumped the throttle forward, praying anything he knocked loose would fall behind the boat, not in it.

The Creek ran due east for a mile, linking Redfish and Coot bays. After 200 yards the mangroves receded, giving way to water oaks. Ben glanced behind to make sure the boat was empty of water moccasins, then slid into the padded seat. The Dusky skimmed through an arched corridor of oak leaves and Spanish moss. Ahead, through a break in the trees, Coot Bay flashed with morning sunlight. Ben scanned the creek for snags and leaned on the throttle. Tree and moss blurred past. Ben squinted, preparing his eyes for the brightness of open water.

The Dusky burst onto a sheet of silver-white glare. Ben raised a hand to shield his eyes from the sun directly in front of him. To his right the water rippled slightly, whether from the morning breeze or a boat's dying wake he couldn't tell. To his left the bay seemed calmer. He angled right, away from the glare and toward the place where Archer would most likely have entered the bay. Was he too late? Ben ground his teeth, tried to make his heart slow, to keep down the sick feeling in his stomach. What if Sam had turned before the bay? His shortcut and second-guessing might have lost Sam. No, he told himself, with Sam so far ahead he was already lost.

The hull vibrated with a staccato rhythm as he edged into the chop. Ben's eyes watered, the wind streaked the tears across his temples and into his ears. He shook his head, glanced to his left. Something glinted across the bay. Something moving, a boat masked by the glare before. Ben sped toward it.

The far shore and the islands merged together in a solid black line, backlit in the morning light. Ben knew of at least three islands on that side of the bay, but couldn't make them out. The other boat disappeared in the shadows there. Ben ducked behind the console, coaxing as much speed as possible from the Dusky. There was, or had been, an old stilt house out that way, on the far side of Graham's Island, one of the few inholdings of private property still left in the Park. The owners visited a week or two every February to escape the Boston winter, and the place sat empty for the rest of the year. Sam could be heading for that. Any farther in that direction Sam would need an airboat to get through the grass flats that spread behind the mangroves. A few narrow channels wound southeast to join the Cheela River, but all were too narrow for the Grady.

Ben throttled back as he neared the island, making sure Sam didn't double back after luring Ben behind across the bay. Sam would be watching, too – if he had stopped there, he would have heard Ben's engine by now. Ben idled around the island, alert for any movement, any sound.

The stilt house was still there, jutting out from a point of high ground, living area and wooden deck suspended above the water, a boathouse underneath. Ben drew even with the house, saw the blunt stern of a pleasure boat tucked into the shadows inside the boathouse. The gold lettering on the twin Mercuries glinted in the reflected light.

Ben put the Dusky in neutral and scanned the boathouse, the house above and the brush around it. Nothing moved. Sam was probably inside. Or watching from the mangroves. Ben let the Dusky drift. Tracking Sam suddenly seemed too easy. Then he recalled the full-throttle chase up the Catahoula, snaking through the narrow channels, and his sheer-luck guess that had barely paid off. Paranoia again. He had used his head, his instincts, and created the break he needed. And this made sense – if anyone became suspicious, the Park superintendent was simply looking in on a little-used house in the Park. And where better to tie up a boat than in a boathouse with a covered dock.

Ben scanned the shore again. Nothing moved. Even the insects were quiet as the day brightened. He still hesitated. He had focused so hard on finding Sam, catching up to him, that he had given little thought to what he would do, what he would say if he actually found Sam. He had no idea how to confront him, but sitting in a skiff in the middle of nowhere would solve nothing.

Ben eased the Dusky up to the boathouse and tied off on a cleat outside where he could step from the bow onto the end of the dock running along one inside wall. The Grady's engines were still pinging from their full-speed run. Ben walked farther in and could smell them, hot and oily, as he passed. He glanced into the boat, froze. It wasn't Sam's boat. Similar, but cluttered with unstowed fishing gear and empty beer cans. Who had he been following?

He jumped at the sound of footsteps behind him. A familiar figure was silhouetted against the boathouse entrance. Will Jenkins, Bailey's brother.

"Hey, Will." Ben relaxed. He stepped forward, hand extended. "Sorry to bust in on you."

"Not sorry enough." Jenkins ignored the hand.
Ben stepped back, bumped into someone else.

"Ol' Ben Gates, gunning through the swamp like he got good sense." Will smiled as he spoke, but his eyes were hard. "What brings you out this far, buddy? Looking for more fires? Looking to set some new ones?"

"It's not like that, Will." Ben tried to turn, see who was behind him. Strong hands forced him to face Jenkins.
"'Course not," Jenkins said. "Just a nasty ol' rumor spread by your enemies, huh? We lost a house in them fires." Will eyed the boathouse ceiling as he spoke. "Stood there and watched, your soldier-boys holding us back." Will stepped toward him, eyes bloodshot. "Then I lost a brother."
"And I lost a friend, Will. But I put an end to Sam's fires." Ben tried again to turn, but Will pulled him back.

"I appreciate that, Ben. We all do. Seeing's how you set 'em."

"No. Will. The Army set them. Archer helped. I stopped them." Had Sam worked so quickly to put the blame on Ben?

"Uh uh, Ben. I got it from the horse's mouth. Said you'd say that, too."

"Horse's ass, if it came from Sam Archer. If I could have saved..."

Will's fist slammed into Ben's jaw. There was the metallic taste of blood and the grit of chipped teeth. Hands grabbed him from behind, held him up, pinned his arms. "Uh uh, boy. You ain't going down that easy." The voice was familiar, but he couldn't place it.

"That was my baby brother." Will leaned close. Ben coughed from bourbon fumes. "You gonna lie about it to my face?" He punched Ben in the stomach. Strong arms pulled Ben upright again. "You killed him. You like fire? You like that swamp, Mr. Lightning Bug?" He punched Ben again. "I'll by-God get you closer to it."

Ben's feet scraped across the dock planks as they dragged him out the boat house and among the stilts supporting the main house. Barely-seen hands slapped duct tape across his mouth. Ben glimpsed wooden support joists above him before someone pulled a pillowcase over his head. He was lifted, carried, then dropped on cool dirt. He kicked, trying to break free.

"Keep him quiet, Toe Jam," Will hissed. "I don't wanna hear him."

Ben knew the other voice then. Todd Jameson, Bailey's friend. Weight pressed on his legs and chest, holding him still. He twisted, tried to yell through the tape. The pillowcase over his head lifted for a moment, then hands shoved an antiseptic-smelling rag over his face. Fumes burned his eyes and nose. The pillowcase world spun. Ben pulled his head away, but the rag pressed tighter against his face. He coughed, gagged. Somewhere far above a deep voice whispered, "Hold it tight, now."

Ben clawed at the dirt with numb hands, clutching the only solid thing he could reach. The earth beneath him dissolved and the voices were gone.

16
—

"*Two-faced little sumbitch.*" *(It was Delmore Moton, liquored up after they turned him loose from Raiford.) "Sneaking around. Playing my boy false. Ben Gates got what was coming – whatever happened to him – him to blame for all that happened to Henry afterwards. To everyone. And Henry was just the one to give it to him. Henry, he never backed down from nothing.*

*"Vengeance may be the Lord's, but Henry took his own, early on, laying Ben out the way he done. Should've walloped him harder, never give him the chance to make trouble later. 'Course, I should've done the same to James Gates the year before – when he first come sniffing around, talking about setting aside old differences."*

*"Not that Henry was blameless, you understand. His fault for trusting a Gates, though I say it as shouldn't. But Ben was in the wrong, no matter how much the Boy Scout he acted later.*

*"See, the Army railroaded Henry for a nut case, but mule-headed and over-loyal is closer to it. Special Forces harnessed that, but they never could control it. It made him*

strong, but it also brought him down. Henry was a good Christian boy, despite his sin of pride. He never dreamed an old friend would take silver for him.

"Hell and half of Georgia could have snuck up on Henry that night, with all the dope and booze and that music rattling the windows. Or what was left of them after he and his buddies got through slinging furniture.

"It was Bailey Jenkins chucked that celadon lamp – the one with the elephant base I brought back from Cam Rahn Bay – smack through the picture window. Damn-near split open Ben's head as he tip-toed towards the house. Would've saved a lot of trouble if it had. As it was, Bailey just wasted a good lamp.

"By the time Henry whacked Bailey down and stuck his head through the window-hole, Ben Gates was at the foot of the steps, peeking under the house at that new SeaRay.

"Henry, too ripped to think straight, he hollered for Ben to get his sorry ass upstairs. With Ben fresh back in town, Henry saw Bailey's replacement – that clean-cut look and college degree made the perfect front man. He thought.

"Ben, though, he had other plans. Him and that Sam Archer. Inside, he picked his way through all the beams, wires, pipes and what all, plywood bowing underfoot the whole time – Henry never was much on the fine finishing work.

"Henry'd perched himself on an ice chest in what was to be the sitting room, pulling on a bottle of Mateus. Bailey Jenkins was laid out on the floor next to him. Bobby Peddiway's bare legs and boots stuck out from behind the couch. *Behind it all was that big, red Mangrove Underground flag tacked up on the beams. SafariLand brochures spread all over the coffee table.*

*Mr. Boy Scout, of course, he knelt next to Bailey, seeing was he OK.*

*"'He's fine!' Henry had to yell over the music. 'And ol' Bobby's just sleeping one off!' He flipped the lid off the ice chest and dug for a beer while Ben stepped to the big stereo cabinet across the room and cut the volume.*

*"'Incoming!' Henry hollered. Ben just did grab the beer flying at his head. Henry took that as a sign from the Lord, delivering Ben's strong right arm to The Cause just in time.*

*"'College ain't ruined your reflexes!' Henry yelled. 'That's good!' He nodded at Bailey Jenkins. 'That Bailey ain't worth a damn! We need you, Bubba.'*

*"He launched into it then, the Spirit moving him, saying more than was good for anyone to hear, with never a thought of first sounding Ben out. I just praise the Lord Henry didn't know more than he did. Things gone to Hell enough as it was.*

*"'We're taking it back, Ben,' Henry said. 'Gonna get this place back to what it was. Do right by the folks that belong here.'*

*"That was a phrase of his – 'do right by the folks.' Where his heart was, too, no matter what some say.*

*"'Yankees invade, expect us to change to their ways. They didn't see they was moving to a fishing town? No, Ben,*

they saw it all and moved in anyway.  Set up that Park to squeeze us out.'

"Ben laughed, treating Henry as stupid-drunk, as Henry tended to get.  As close as those boys had been, they'd drifted while Ben was away.  He couldn't see Henry was serious, with a purpose and a mission.

"For his part, Henry couldn't see Ben had grown two-faced as his daddy.  Only he was fishing for Archer, not James Gates.  And as bad as James Gates was, Sam Archer was worse.  I don't claim to be guiltless, you understand.  I trusted James Gates after growing up with him.  But Ben, he'd just met that Archer.

"That boy was blinded by ambition.  And a selfish pride in his own works he tried to keep hid.  Henry had no idea Archer'd already got to Ben, preyed on that.  A serpent more subtle than any beast of the field was Archer.  Twisted Ben around so all he could see was that fancy Park job and finally coming off the hero.

"See, Ben had been gone too long to notice the foreigners moving in, bitching about crab traps.  Even now they don't want to see real, honest, working ones under our houses, but they're damn-quick to set a new mailbox on a stack of varnished ones.  And order a plate of claws down at Sharky's.

"'They're escapists, pure and simple,' Henry said that night, 'and I don't hold with that.  Nothing I hate worse than a liar.'

"Thing is, as smart as Henry was, the goodness in him made him see only the goodness in others. That's what tripped him up with the Airborne, got him hustled out as a Section Eight. Tripped him up with Ben, too.

"Ben took advantage of that. He'd seen that new SeaRay. He'd seen that new, big-ass stereo. He played curious, drew Henry out.

"Now, in fairness, I don't believe Ben knew his own daddy was bankrolling Henry.

"As for Henry, all he knew was his best friend's daddy had a sympathetic ear and wanted to help on the sly. And his best friend himself was back from school, sounding interested and eager. Before he knew it, Henry was explaining about the Mangrove Underground.

"Ben laughed, working Henry. Called the mangrove on the flag a broccoli with tentacles. 'You'll stir up more trouble than you can handle,' he said.

"That's when Henry's mouth, and that Mateus, got the best of him. 'All is vanity, said the Preacher,' and that was Henry all over. He knew he couldn't mention James Gates, not without James' say-so. But he spilled all their ideas, desperate to get Ben to see the logic.

"Yankees were swarming in, Henry said. Cheap land and no taxes was drawing them. 'Lack of natural predators,' was how he always put it. Mangrove Underground'd change that – bunch of wild-eyed Southern boys tearing things up, making life difficult, pretty soon the transplants'd all be packing up, heading back north, warning their friends off.

"There was to be no violence, you understand. That was never Henry's way. Or mine. He aimed to stir enough commotion to kill the Park, make the Yankees realize they weren't in their nice, safe cities no more.

"I can still hear him, launching into that mumbojumbo of his about 'exerting moral influence.' Henry was into that Japanese crap. They fed it to him at OCS. 'Expendable agents and nine-layered heavens.' Load of Kwai-Chang Caine bullshit, but it worked for him. And he did right for himself, at the end. Burned half that damn Park. They never caught him, neither, so that says something, too.

"That night, though, Ben had heard enough. He chucked Henry's drivers license on the table. Henry, he went silent, knowing the only place Ben could've got it. And knowing the only reason Ben'd be out that far in the sticks.

"'Guy named Archer like to have found that, up Tarpon Creek,' Ben said, slick as could be. To his credit, now, Henry didn't move, waiting to see what that Ben would do next. 'Wanted to keep it between us,' Ben said, playing to the hilt.

"Like I said, Henry saw the best in people. Took Ben at his word. And that Ben had thrown in with him. 'The lips of a fool will swallow himself up,' the Scriptures say, and, sure enough, Henry jumped from his ideas to his actual plans: Where they'd hide in the Park, where they'd strike from. That was what that burned chickee was about. Announcing their presence. They had backers, secret financiers to make Third World countries proud. If Ben didn't join in, then he was by-God a traitor to everything he held dear.

"Henry never would see the only loyalty any Gates ever had

was to himself. And Ben would never see it was our way of life against theirs, no matter how many times, how many ways any of us explained it.

"No, Sam Archer and his damn Park had already took hold. 'Wilderness preservation,' hell. Taking that land to make the Park was at the heart of all the evil. Still is. It's what drew the Yankees to start with, gave them a Scotch-Guarded wilderness with gates and rangers and walking trails. They come down for that, built the houses they could never afford up in Yankeeland, and made sure no one built nearby.

"The plan James Gates fed us all (excepting Henry) was to flood the market with houses that wouldn't sell, and drop property values so local folks could afford things again. Free that Park land up for something useful. Take Hermosa County back.

"Henry didn't know his jack-off Mangrove Underground was a part of James Gates' bigger schemes. James figured if the cops was busy hunting lightning bugs in the swamp, they wouldn't be watching James, me or the others. Of course, James told none of us how big his real plans was. Or how he'd make a killing when all was said and done. Problem was, while the cops was watching Henry, that Archer was watching all of us.

"Still, it wasn't Archer's fault, or James Gates', or mine that Henry went the way he did. That blame lies square on Ben's shoulders. Chose to do what he did. Burn his own people.

"That night, though, the more Henry talked, and the more sincere he got, the more Ben baited him, begging him not to go through with things, sucking out all the information he could. 'Sounds dangerous,' he said. 'How, exactly, could anything like that work?'

"Ben was too smart for himself, though. Henry may have been a blind idealist, but he wasn't dumb. Ben overplayed his hand. Told Henry no one would egg on such nonsense unless they meant Henry harm. He was fishing for a name, but that may have been the only truthful thing Ben said all night. Or in his life. It's also what set off the chain reaction that ruined all of us, in short order.

"Henry paused, kicking over all the doubts he'd pushed aside – why would James Gates do so much to help a Moton? Could something this wild really work? Why would James Gates give him so much money?

"Henry sat down, all quiet of a sudden, letting things settle in his head. He knew then he'd been had. And he'd said too much, to the wrong person. But the truth had set him free – he had to slip loose of Ben, get up-close and personal with James Gates, beat the truth out of him if he had to.

"And even then Ben and Henry might have talked things out peaceful. But Ben went and called Henry crazy. Henry wasn't – the tests proved that – but folks repeating a thing like that gets to a man.

"Henry did it slick. I'll give him that. The Lord taught his hands to war and his fingers to fight. Apologized for being drunk, for babbling nonsense. Thanked Ben for talking sense to him. He stood and held out his hand, to make up. When Ben reached to shake, Henry snatched him forward. Knee-in-the-gut, foot-in-the-jewels. Boom! Boom! Just like that.

"Mr. Boy Scout landed on his all-fours. Tried to get up, and Henry cold-cocked him upside the head with that Mateus bottle. Even then, Henry didn't mean Ben any real harm – just laid him out and left him there. Anybody else he'd have worked over proper. Like that Airborne major that raised such a stink after Henry had to smack him.

"By the time Ben came to and dragged himself out the door, Henry had hooked that boat trailer to his truck and was headed down the drive. Slashed Ben's tires, too, before he left. All Ben could do was lean against the corner post and watch Henry's tail lights fade.

"Next time those boys seen each other was at the old barge next night. Everybody knows that story, or versions of it. Needless. Shameful. Too many folks with proud looks and lying tongues. And Ben Gates at the heart of it.

"Got his just reward, though. Then, and later. Or so I reckon. Henry, his failing was being so kind-hearted. Of course, again, I say that as shouldn't."

## 17

A vibration pulsed through him, a sound and a feeling all at once. There was a rocking, too, a steady back-and-forth motion in time with the throb in his head and stomach. Darkness. He lay on his back. His throat burned, dry. Something soft, a cloth, covered his face. The pillowcase, Ben remembered. He smelled a hint of whatever they had used to knock him out. He smelled water, too, the muddy odor of the deep swamp, and fiberglass, and something else. Gasoline. Or two-cycle exhaust. The vibration took on an outboard's drone. A small engine, working hard. He was in a boat. A skiff, probably. His head hurt. His stomach rolled. Ben tried to turn onto his side, but his body didn't move.

"He's coming around," a cold voice by his feet hissed.

"Almost there." Will Jenkins' voice boomed above him.

Ben squirmed again, felt his body respond this time. He rolled onto his side and lifted a hand to his mouth to peel away the tape before he vomited. Something slammed into the small of his back.

"Lie quiet, asshole!" Toe Jam's voice sounded close to his ear.

Ben rolled onto his stomach, sliding a hand to his mouth as he rolled. The duct tape came off slowly, tearing at his lips and unshaved stubble. Ben tried to relax, slow his breathing, save his strength. No telling where Will and the others were taking him, or what they had planned. Rough him up, drop him off in the middle of nowhere, probably. They were friends. Or acquaintances, anyway. People he'd grown up with. Good people, just angry. He moved one foot. It slid freely. They hadn't taped his feet. That said something good about their plans. He could use that. Maybe. If he could stop the throbbing in his head and stomach.

The outboard's tone dropped. The rocking changed tempo as the skiff slowed. They idled back, and Ben felt the slight catch as Will dropped the engine into neutral.

"This'll do," Will said. Boots shuffled next to Ben's head. Someone snatched the pillowcase away, sending a rush of fresh air across his face.

Ben pulled his knees under him, ready to jump or run. All he could see at first were faint pinpricks in the darkness. Stars, he realized. Leo's head curved low, Regulus glittering above the horizon. The skiff was pointed southeast, a detached part of him realized. It was well past midnight for the constellation to be visible. Hands shook him, cutting short his thoughts.

"Up and at 'em, Natureboy." The cold voice again. A pale face, skeletal, yet familiar, appeared in the dark, lit by a flashlight held low. Delmore Moton. He yanked Ben up to one of the bench seats. "Time to meet the swamp." His low monotone sounded distant.

"Or what you left of it." Will's face appeared to Ben's right.

"Where...?" Ben clutched the gunwale as the boat rocked. Toe Jam's feet shuffled behind him in the skiff's bow. Ben hadn't realized Delmore Moton was out of prison. His presence here was a bad sign.

"Cavalier Bay, Buckwheat." Will jabbed him in the chest.

Ben looked around. Cavalier was deep in the backcountry. There was a seldom-used campsite on the southeast shore where the spring runs emptied into the bay, but he saw no campfire. There was nothing else near the bay. Except alligators, drawn by the constant flow of fresh water. Were they going to the ground site? If they left him there, it could be days before campers came by.

"Will, you don't have to do this."

"Oh, nobody has to do anything, boy," Delmore Moton said. "We all make choices." He took a long pull from a bottle of Old Grand Dad, then passed the bottle to Toe Jam. "Like your daddy setting me up. Like you betraying my boy." Ben strained to hear the lifeless voice.

"I didn't, Mr. Moton..."

"Like you dropping Bailey in the middle of your fire," Will Jenkins cut in.

"I carried him out!" They were drunk, but he could talk to them, explain. "The Army set the fires. For Sam Archer."

"Uh-uh." Will jabbed him in the chest again. "Last thing Bailey told me was what you done, how the whole town'd've gone up if it weren't for Sam Archer."

174

"Archer called in the Army!" The words came out too high, too fast. Where would a near-death Bailey come up with that? "Will, you know me. We all..."

Will's punch knocked him backwards. "My brother's a liar? You kill him, burn us all out, and you ain't got the balls to admit it to my face? No, Ben, I don't know you!" Delmore Moton and Toe Jam muttered agreement.

A chill swept through him. Their minds were made up. Talking would change nothing, but talking was the only chance he had. Will stood over him, fists clenched, ready to hit him again. At least he could get a punch in. Ben tried to stand, take a swing, but a numbness spread through his legs, paralyzing him.

"You ain't even got the balls to do anything about me saying you got no balls! Archer was right. You are a spine-less little piece of shit, ain't you?"

"'Spine' makes you pick a three-on-one fight?" His voice was still too high. Sam had publicly blamed Ben for the fires, then. And used Bailey to spread that rumor, wind up Will and the others.

"No, Buckwheat, this's just plain fun," Will said. "Been dreamin' on this for years." Delmore Moton's cold voice never changed tone. "You ain't your daddy, but you're close enough."

Ben saw himself lunging, knocking Will or Moton over the side, holding them under water. They were going to leave him out here, anyway. He could take one of them with him, then swim to shore. Ben shifted his feet. Something slammed into his back, knocking him forward. Arms slipped under his shoulders and pulled him upright.

"Hold him there, Toe Jam." Will took the whisky from Delmore Moton. "You know, Ben, we come out here tonight wanting to beat king hell out of you." He took a long pull from the bottle, then tapped it against the side of Ben's head. "But standing here now, listening to you piss and moan, you ain't worth hurting my hands or scuffing my boat."

Ben gritted his teeth, trying to will away the numbness. Why couldn't he move, punch, act without thinking? Maybe Will would take him back to town now that he'd had his say and scared Ben.

Delmore Moton stared at him, cheeks sunken, shadowed eye sockets like black holes. He pulled a second flashlight from a storage bin, gave Ben a toothy grin.

"There's others out here ain't so forgiving." Moton panned the beam across the water. A dozen orange embers glowed in the light. Alligators, with only their eyes above the water reflecting the glare. Moton played the light around the boat, showing orange eyes on all sides. "Now, son, I remember you saying, 'I'm part of this place.' You remember that? Think them gators agree?" The voice was colder than ever.

Toe Jam chuckled behind him.

The numbness overwhelmed Ben. He knew it then for what it was – the emptiness surging up again, eager to suck him down. He couldn't let them know he was afraid. "Mr. Moton, don't do this." There was a pleading tone in his voice he had never heard, had never imagined before. In that moment he hated himself more than he had ever hated anyone or anything.

"Will, you wanna take this boy back to town?"

"We could do." Will and Toe Jam laughed. "Or not." Ben had to do something. He made himself go limp, pulling Toe Jam forward. Then he kicked out, aiming for Will's crotch. Will dodged, started to fall, but caught himself on the outboard. Toe Jam shoved Ben down, slamming Ben's knees to the fiberglass hull. At the same time, Delmore Moton's fist swung up into Ben's stomach, doubling him over. They lifted him, rolled him across the gunwales. He sank beneath the water, struggling for air, not sure which way was up. He thrashed to the surface. The skiff floated in front of him, maybe three feet away.

"Can't start no fires or spread no lies about Mr. Archer out there, can you, son?" Will was laughing. In the bow, Toe Jam stood, bourbon bottle in one hand, canoe paddle in the other. Ben reached for the boat. Toe Jam smiled and held out the paddle.

"Thanks, Todd," Ben said.

Toe Jam spat and thrust the paddle at Ben's head. Ben managed to swing a hand up to deflect it. "You go commune with the swamp now, boy," Toe Jam yelled. "Talk to your people for us."

Will Jenkins put the outboard in gear and spun the skiff away.

"Hey! You can't leave me here!" Ben yelled. They wouldn't leave him in the water. They just wanted to scare him. Anger, fear, and anger at the fear blended together, giving him strength.

"The wheels of the Lord grind exceedingly small, now don't they, boy?" Delmore Moton gave a wisp of a grin. Will Jenkins gunned the motor, and the skiff lurched away into the darkness.

Ben tread water, trying to think, to stay calm. He had to get to shore. There were alligators all around him. "Gators got no reason to go after you," his father's voice echoed from long ago, "unless you're thrashing like a hurt animal." It had made sense when Ben was 10 and safe on shore. But now, in the dark water on a moonless night, he wasn't so sure. He imagined alligators, big ones, gliding closer, slipping beneath him.

His hand bumped something and he jerked away. Seconds later the slick feel of a floating branch registered in his mind. He yelled again, hoping the men would come back. Of course they'd come back. He yelled until he could no longer hear the outboard. He was shaking, Ben realized. He was alone, in darkness. He would get no help. He could do nothing to stop an alligator from grabbing him, pulling him under.

The paralyzing fear returned. And the self-loathing that went with it. This was weakness and did him no good. It did no good for anyone. It was an inherent flaw, the personal failing that left him impotent in any crisis. His mom had died because of it. His dad, too. It had made Kelly, and Henry, betray him. Now the Morehouses were dead because of it as well. He deserved this.

A logical part of his mind told him to swim, slow and steady, and hope for the best. The fear, the hesitation were more deadly than any alligator. But which way? Clouds were thickening to the west, blotting out the stars. To his right, though, Regulus, and the rest of Leo, were still clear. That was southeast, toward the Cavalier campsite. Dry ground instead of a tangle of mangrove roots. There might even be campers. He tread higher in the water, eager for the wink of firelight, but saw nothing.

Ben forced a numb, tentative stroke in that direction, not daring to reach too far. His stomach ached from Will's punches. The semi-circle of stars ahead was his only guide. He wondered if Will had cut the motor, was quietly paddling back to pick him up. He shut out that thought. They weren't coming back. Swimming was his only hope, the only thing he could control. He kicked hard, swung his arms forward in a front crawl to reach shore as quickly as possible. Muddy water splashed into his eyes and mouth. Ben coughed, stopped swimming, afraid his splashing would draw alligators. Afraid of what his flailing arms might hit. He imagined gators floating just in front of him, mouths open, waiting to grab his arms as they splashed down. He switched to a modified breaststroke, keeping his face above water and easing his hands forward slightly, then pulling them back in short, ragged strokes.

Ben swam. He had no idea how long or how far. He gave up counting strokes at 100, when the rising count became depressing. His only gauge of time was Leo's steady climb against the clouds advancing from behind him.

He had to reach shore before they blotted out his guide stars. Alligators were all around him, Ben knew. They had crowded around the skiff, and unless his swimming had scared them off, they were just as close now. Or closer. He couldn't think of that.

His father's voice echoed in his head again. Ben listened at first, as a distraction, then began to silently talk back. He could have been watching a cartoon of himself swimming, with a steady commentary running in his head. He realized he was singing something to himself. "*Scooby Doo, where are you...*" his voice rasped in time with his strokes. The water's thick mud taste filled his mouth.

"Steady, son," his dad's voice said. "Slow and steady. They won't hurt you."

"You better be right," Ben said. He knew better, but ignored that. He focused on each stroke. A slow pull, a kick, and a glide that lasted forever. His arms ached. His legs, weighted with jeans and boots, pulled at him like sea anchors. His stomach and ribs burned, as if Will had broken something or knocked something loose inside.

Something brushed past his hand. Ben thrashed forward several strokes before he could stop the panic. Splashing would make things worse. It could have been another branch, a fish... anything. Swimming slowly and steadily was his only chance. Shore had to be close. "Just a branch," he said to himself. The spoken words calmed him, though he wasn't sure why. "Or a big tarpon. Right?" He pulled harder. He was almost there.

"Flail like that, you wear yourself out in no time." His father's voice was close, as close as it had been on the dock years before. He spun, looked behind him, but there was only darkness. The clouds had crept even with Leo's head. Ben swam harder.

"Have to make shore. While there's stars." His voice came in ragged bursts.

"Water's bigger, stronger than you'll ever be, son." The voice reached him from 20 years before. "You fight it, it'll beat you every time."

Ben shook his head. His dad was gone. He would get no help there. The voice, or memory or whatever it was, was right, though. He had no idea how far the shore was. If he tired himself out now, he might not make it. And while an alligator might avoid a swimming person, it would certainly go for a floating one.

"Slow and steady," he said to himself. "Slow and steady."

His arms dragged. His stomach and ribs burned with every stroke. He slowed, lengthened his glides, trying to rest his arms.

"Atta boy! Easy does it gets you there."

"I know! I am!" Imagined or not, the voice was annoying.

"Getting mad won't help. Concentrate. Glide. Pull and glide."

Ben ignored the voice, pushed away thoughts of alligators and focused on each stroke. Pull, kick and glide, his mouth just above water level. Pull, kick and glide. He needed to rest, just for a minute. One minute wouldn't hurt. The alligators wouldn't close in that fast. Ben rolled to his back, let his arms and legs dangle. If he could get some feeling back in his arms, make his ribs stop hurting, he would be alright.

"No time for that, son."

Ben ignored the voice. He had to rest. It was nice to have the company, though.

Voices carried across the water from somewhere behind him. Ben raised his head, held his breath to make sure. East, toward what remained of Leo, he heard faint laughter. A woman's laughter.

"Hey!" Ben tread as high as he could. "Over here!" He couldn't see lights, but someone was out there, camping or fishing. "Hey!" He swam toward the voices, looking for a glimmer of light, anything.

"Over here! I'm here!" His voice came rougher with every yell. He paused, tiring again. He could wait here for them. A man said something, and the woman laughed again, faint and to his right. Ben turned, swam toward them.

"Hey! Heeeyy!" The yell wasn't as loud as he had hoped. It didn't matter. The people were too caught up in their conversation to notice him. "Damn it! Over here!" He swam again. He had to get closer.

"Little more," he whispered to himself. "A little more and you're good." His hands were numb. His legs ached. Knives tore in his midsection. Ben paused, listening.

He shivered, tried to stop, and shivered again. He had been in the water too long. He had to find land, dry off, and get warm. He was so tired, though. Ben took a deep breath and floated, letting his arms and legs dangle for a moment. A moment was all he needed.

"He's still out there, swimming." A woman's voice, familiar, and so close.

"He'll miss supper he don't get in soon." It could have been his dad. Again. It didn't matter who it was, or who they were talking about.

Ben kicked toward them. Something bumped his side. Ben felt raised knobs on whatever it was slide beneath him, through the spot where he had been.

"Damn! Hey! Help! Here!" They had to hear him. They were close, and looking for a swimmer. "I'm here!" He thrashed ahead with what energy he had left.

"Hurry up, Ben. You're late." His mother's voice. The other swimmer was named Ben, too? No. This made no sense, these voices without people. He had imaged his dad's voice, so why not a couple of campers? Leo and Regulus were gone, lost behind the clouds. Which way was east? He could have been swimming in circles chasing the imaginary voices. Something welled up inside him. Anger, he realized. He couldn't quit.

"Think, Ben. Think," he said. Clouds covered the stars. Shore could be anywhere. The voices, real or imagined, had come from that direction while Leo had been visible. He should still be on course. His brain could be giving it's own cues, intuition guiding him. Or he was too chilled to think clearly. In front of him now he made out a faint glow, the rising moon behind thin clouds, maybe.

"Swim toward the moon, you crazy bastard." Swamp water filled his mouth with the taste of mud and decay. Ben gagged, fought to keep afloat. He dog-paddled, keeping his mouth above water. The moon brightened. Shore had to be that way. There had been no moon the night before, though, while he talked to reporters until dawn. There should be none this night, either. A lantern, then? He blinked to clear his eyes. The light disappeared. The panic he had fought back before surged up again, stronger. He had imagined the light, as he had imagined the voices. Ben stopped, exhausted. Afraid. This wasn't right. Shore could be any direction. He floated in a featureless dark, trying to think. If he couldn't think, he would die.

"No, Ben! Hurry! Hurry!" His mom's voice came from his right, where the light had been, so clear and so close she could have been in the water beside him.

Ben swam away. If he died out here, it wouldn't be from chasing ghosts. He shivered again. He couldn't feel his arms or legs. His chest felt prickly, cold. The beatings, the time in the water, the exertion - all were catching up with him. It didn't matter. His panic eased, was replaced by something else. Disgust. He deserved this. After all the hurt he had caused his friends, his family, his town, he deserved this. An ache inside, festering for years, burst out then, drowning out the physical pain of his stomach and ribs. All his life, all he had ever done, had led him to this situation. For everything he had ever done, he deserved this. "Ben! *This way*! Please!" The voice was still to his right and behind him slightly.

Why should the voice care? It didn't matter. His lungs hurt. He tried to stop shivering but couldn't. He couldn't feel his arms or legs. He wouldn't reach shore. Ben rolled onto his back again, closed his eyes. Alligators usually stuffed their prey under sunken logs to rot until they could tear off chunks small enough to swallow. No one would find him. Or miss him.

A calmness came then. This was all inevitable, and had been long before Will and the others dumped him here. This had been inevitable since he decided to go along with Sam's scheme, maybe even before that. Will Jenkins had been right, though. He was part of the swamp now, as much as his mom or his dad. Ben smiled at that, comforted to feel so close to his parents again. Maybe that was why he was hearing their voices now. Of course, neither his mom nor her spirit people had been much help this time, either. He laughed. The Nunnehi again. Well, why not? If they were out here, they would be laughing, too. Ben felt himself floating above the bay, watching gators crowd around a still object bobbing in the water. Him. He saw them nosing closer, spiraling up from beneath him, like some old movie poster. It would be quick. He closed his eyes and waited. It was OK.

Water rippled to his right. Something bumped against him, grabbed his elbow gently, almost tenderly. He had thought it would be more violent than that.

"Rest easy, bud." A man's voice, familiar. It was starting again. His brain making things easier for him. "Gonna help me swim?" What could it hurt, playing along? The distraction was almost pleasant.

"No, bud. You're through swimming."

A nice touch. The Angel of Death was an alligator. Gabriel? Michael? His mom would have known. Maybe her voice would jump in and tell him. "It doesn't matter," he laughed.

"Yeah. Well, you got one more good kick, help haul you up?"

Something gripped his shoulders, the world spun, and the darkness was complete.

## 18

*"You're naïve, Godzilla." He meant it ugly.*

*Like he could talk, stuffed in the patrol car beside me. Then bolting when they cut him loose. Like he was the only one mattered. I mean, a monkey would've known they'd follow him.*

*The detective, Fielding, was slick. Firing the same questions at him over and over, winding Ben out. Man, by the end of it, I was ready to answer the questions.*

*"Where's Mr. Moton?"*

*"What's your relationship with Miss Barnes?"*

*"How do you know Mr. Jenkins, here?"*

*And Ben. Playing stupid. Rattling off a bogus list of places Henry might have gone, but where any idiot knew he hadn't.*

*I'd have backhanded him, but for the cuffs. And the glow-in-the-dark spikes jabbing me forward so I could barely breathe.*

*Fielding just smiled. Played dumb right back. Like Ben's crap smelled like roses.*

*All Ben wanted was to blast out of there, go Luke Skywalker with Kelly. Like she needed help. He was so amped up when Fielding let him go that he never bothered to check his rearview. Or notice the boats and copters dogging him, obvious as shit.*

*Anyway, crammed in beside him, I thanked him for the 'naïve.' He looked me over like I was a pinhead. A compliment. It's sweet when the smart ones screw themselves. See, I'd watched him slide through the crowd. Right to the cop cars flashing all red and blue across the park gates and all those faces. Hoping to blend with the tourist mob. About the time he hit the crime scene tape, I heard Fielding say to old Wilson, "... address on Mr. Moton." Ben heard that, too, 'cause he tensed up just then.*

*"Someone stole a mermaid!" a tourist woman yelled. Ben went bug-eyed.*

*It's scary what a Cuervo breakfast'll get you into. It was a gas when Henry explained it. Put on the dinosaur suit. Cannonball into the show. Scare the girls, spread the Mangrove Underground flag, run like hell. Tourists would freak.*

*But I damn-near drowned in that stupid costume. The flag wound around me so tight I couldn't move my arms or legs. They had to peel it off me after they yanked me out.*

*Henry was no help – he was in the dressing room by then. He never planned to snatch Kelly. Not that he mentioned, anyway. He was spontaneous like that. Steal a romantic afternoon, pass it off as eco-terrorism.*

*Back then, man, me and Henry were drinking TNT and smoking dynamite. Immortal. Goddamn giants in our own time.*

*Ben's problem was he thought he was, too. Seriously. That's why Henry had to windmill him – like whacking a TV to get the picture to come clear. Percussive maintenance, you know?*

*Life's too short for posers. Spend too much time with one, next thing you know, you're one, too. That's the big fear, man. And that was Ben. All over. Figures he'd be a boss-man later.*

*But yeah, Henry'd gone aggro on him the night before. Ben was gunning for him. He'd seen the flag. And the Rap-Tor schedule. Then, listening to the crowd, he knew what happened. Ben edged away, digging for car keys.*
*"There! Ben Gates!" Wilson yelled. "He'd know!"*

*Ben played 'possum-in-the-headlights'. Fielding motioned, and two cops pulled Ben under the yellow tape.*

*Fielding eyed Ben's fresh shiner, the muddy clothes, three-day growth. "Nasty bruise, Mr. Gates," he said. "And fresh." He talked like that, man. He'd crack your skull stuffing you in a patrol car, then say, "Sorry, Mr. Jenkins."*

*Anyway, Ben played dumb. No great reach. "I fell in the skiff." Just like that. "Off a chickee I was fixing."*

*"Uh- huh," said Fielding. "Mr. Wilson here says you know Miss Barnes."*

*"What happened to Kelly?" He said it too fast. Fielding almost smiled, just for a second.*

*He let Ben squirm. "Where were you about an hour ago, Mr. Gates?"*

*"Not kidnapping my girlfriend!" Ben was amped, overplaying it.*

"Girlfriend?" Fielding raised an eyebrow. He glanced at Wilson, then at me. We both shrugged. Fielding pulled Ben away from the crowd. "I don't believe in coincidence, do you, Mr. Gates?"

"It wasn't me."

"I thought it was, you'd be in cuffs. With Mr. Jenkins." Fielding nodded toward the patrol car, toward me in that jack-off dinosaur suit. I'd've waved if I could've.

Ben saw me then for the first time. He looked at the rubber Godzilla head next to me, then back at me. He just stared for three, maybe four seconds. Then he busted out laughing. I laughed, too. I mean, what else was there to do, really?

"I take it you know Mr. Jenkins?" Fielding said.

"Bailey jumped in like that and grabbed Kelly?" Asshole could barely talk he was laughing so hard.

"Mr. Jenkins jumped in," Fielding nodded at me, "while someone else abducted Miss Barnes. I need that other person."

Ben stopped mid-laugh.

Fielding waved his notepad. "Two people I want to talk to are you and a... Mr. Henry Moton."

Ben kept a poker face, watching Fielding's eyes. Fielding nodded. "Where's Mr. Moton, Ben?"

Man, for once in his life, Ben said nothing. I have no idea what was going through that weasel-brain, but you could tell he wasn't about to nark on Henry. He wanted Henry for himself.

*Fielding saw it, too. "Ever been to jail, Mr. Gates?"*

*Ben's head jerked up like he'd been bitch-slapped. All kinds of yahoos have all kinds of ideas what Ben was up to back then: how much he knew, who he was covering for. But right there, with him standing beside the cop car, all I saw was a dude wanting a swing at Henry.*

*You could see the wheels turning. He had to give out enough to make Fielding happy, but still beat him to Henry. I mean, by then Ben knew damn-well Henry was at the old barge. Only a few of us knew about it from when we were kids, and me sitting there was a dead giveaway.*

*Ben drooped his shoulders, looking all beat-down. "Could be a dozen places," he said. Fielding smiled and pulled out a pen. That's when Ben rattled off all the bogus hideouts, dropping Coot Bay in like it was an afterthought, covering his butt. And never once looking over at me.*

*Fielding read the list back, place-by-place, asking Ben why Henry would be at each. Except then he wasn't writing anything. He just watched Ben, seeing how he answered.*

*In between he'd throw in a "When's the last time you saw Miss Barnes?" And "How do you know Miss Barnes?" Always, "Miss Barnes."*

*And Ben correcting him with, "Kelly," and amping up more every time. Insisting they were girlfriend-boyfriend. I almost felt sorry for the guy.*

*So Fielding went through the list three, maybe four times. Ben started answering with, "Like I told you...," his tone all nasty. And glancing toward the crowd, toward the parking lot. Two cops slid up on either side of him. Fielding got tired of messing with him and stuffed him in the back seat with me.*

*"Nice suit,' Ben said after they shut the door. Swear to God that was the best he could do.*

*"Nice face," I said. And, "Kelly's fine." Being nice, smoothing things over.*

*That's when he made the 'naïve' crack. I shut up, let the asshole stew. You can only do so much sometimes. Especially when someone's so smart they're stupid, you know?*

*"They at the barge?" He tried to work me.*

*"Dunno, dude," I said. "Naïve. Remember?"*

*His face was good and red by then. Started talking to himself. "Not right," he muttered at first. Silence, then, "... broke the rules." I don't think he even knew he was talking. I mean, he was going bat-shit right beside me, uncuffed and unrestrained, and no way for me to move if he went mental. I yelled for them to get me out of there.*

*Fielding stuck his head in the window. Never been so happy to be face-to-face with a cop in my life. "Mr. Gates? Your father James Gates?"*

*Ben shut up for maybe three seconds. Like Fielding'd whacked him with a board. "Yeah." He said it like he was ready for a fight.*

*Fielding nodded. "He ever mention Mr. Moton?" "Not since high school," Ben's voice kind of shook as he said it.*

*Fielding smiled. "Straightest answer I had all day."
He opened the door and motioned Ben out. "Thank you for
your help Mr. Gates. Don't wander too far."*

*Ben gave me one last go-to-hell look and bolted, trying
to walk slow, like he was in no hurry. Fielding grinned big
as shit at the cop next to him.*

*Then, just as Ben ducked under the yellow tape,
Sam Archer, the Parks guy, was just there, totally blocking
his way.*

*"Ben! Good to see you! What happened?" Archer
half-yelled. Then he pulled Ben close, whispered something,
and stepped back and half-yelled again, "Sorry to hear it.
They'll find her, though!"*

*Ben shoved people out of the way then and ran for
that old rust-bucket LeMans of his. He tore back through
town, to his house, too strung out to think of looking back.
Straight to the Dusky. Tore out to save the princess.
And of course they followed him.*

## 19

Darkness. A man's voice. Then his mom's. Pain shot through his hand. He twisted away from serpents coiling bright-toothed around him. The man's voice returned, singing or chanting. Ben knew the voice. Who? The one who spoke as he swam, yet more familiar. Angel or devil or swamp spirit, Ben forced open his eyes to see.

Orange light flickered. Fire. Warmth to his left. A low canopy curved down to form a wall to his right. No one in sight. No voices. A faint crackle from the fire. The canopy rippled in an unfelt breeze, like something exhaling in its sleep. Ben squinted at the woven surface, dark green in the firelight. Canvas. Hell was trimmed with green canvas. To his left, beyond the canopy's edge, interwoven branches fluttered with a deeper orange. A campsite then, not the afterlife. He lay beneath a crude lean-to in a clearing under the mangroves, their leaves blocking most of the sky. Tones, like wind chimes, but continuous, rang in his ears. Strange lights, fireflies maybe, flickered among the leaves. Stars, with branches waving in front of them, he realized. A bright star, with three fainter ones beside it. He knew them, but couldn't think of their names.

Ben rolled his head to the left. Something blocked his view. His fingers slid along taut canvas, felt poles running along his sides. A cot, its center sagging and its frame curling up, holding him in place and limiting his sight. A familiar scratchiness clawed at his skin as he moved. A thin wool military surplus blanket, like the ones his dad hadalways taken camping.

Ben pulled the blanket tighter, suddenly cold despite the fire and the warm night. He was alive. He didn't know who had saved him or why. He didn't care. Somehow he was safe and far from alligators. Panic rushed back. He tried to sit up, see the ground beneath him. He could barely raise his head, though he shook with the effort.

"You pissed them ol' boys off good," a deep voice rumbled behind him.

"Yeah," the word scratched in Ben's throat. His voice was barely a whisper. "Joke got out of hand."

"Some joke."

The voice in the darkness. But more than that. Ben knew the man. From long ago, maybe, but he knew him. He tried to turn his head to see the man's face.

"Lie still. You used up seven, maybe eight lives out there."

Ben closed his eyes. He couldn't move anyway. "Thanks. Could use someone on my side."

"Ain't on your side. Just ain't gonna watch anybody get chomped like that."

"Where..." The trees, or something, were wrong. There should be more open sky. "This isn't Cavalier."

"Where don't matter." There was a noise that could have been a cough, or a brief laugh.

Fear rushed through Ben again. The man said he had nothing to do with Will Jenkins, but... "You just happened to be out here?" The words were out before Ben realized. He tensed. The man had carved a hidden campsite under the mangroves in the backcountry. There were few legal reasons anyone would do that.

"I was here."

"Lucky for me. Thanks again." Ben hesitated, not wanting to push, but still curious. Still hoping for an ally. "I know you, don't I?"

A rumbling laugh came from behind him. "Bubba, you don't know yourself, much less anyone else. But yeah, we've met."

The man stepped into view. Matted hair, trying to be dreadlocks, hung level with his shoulders. The skin around his eyes looked pale above a dark beard. A camouflaged canvas bush jacket hung across broad shoulders. But the eyes were what held Ben's attention. Pale blue, they seemed to glow amid the dark hair hiding most of the man's face. Ben knew the eyes, their intensity. The intense face in the crowd at the post firefight press conference. The man leaned close.

"Course, last time we talked, we was both a bit preoccupied." He grinned. "Damn-near knocked you down with your daddy on my shoulders."

Ben closed his eyes again. He was hallucinating. He had drowned, been eaten, and his mind was trying to make sense of his brain's last twitches. Henry Moton had died years ago. Was this some backwoods purgatory? He opened his eyes. Henry was still there, grinning. Ben knew the smile, though it seemed less threatening than he remembered.

"No, you ain't dreaming. You ain't dead, either. Come close, though. Had a hell of a time pulling your sorry ass out of that slough."

"Your dad..."

"Don't know about me. He and I'll talk later."

Ben shook his head, trying to clear it. It was Henry, but how? Behind Henry, the bright star and its companions flashed golden-white through the leaves. "You can't have been out here ten years."

"'Course not." Henry's eyes lost their focus then, as if he were looking past Ben, or through him. "Not *here*, exactly."

Ben laughed to himself. Dream or hallucination or whatever it was, it seemed harmless. "Hiding in the Mangrove Underground?"

"Underground, yeah. So to speak." Henry's eyes drifted back into focus. "Important thing, I was here when your buddies roared up and dumped you off." He patted Ben's shoulder. The hand felt solid, warm. But if the man was real, this couldn't be Henry. And if it was Henry... but there was more that didn't make sense.

"Where are the others?"

"Hell and gone. Never looked back."

"No. The man and woman. Looking for their kid."
Henry looked puzzled. "Nobody out there but you and me,
Bubba. And more gators than you want to think about."

"Right." Ben closed his eyes again. "And here I thought it
was the Nunnehi saved me."

"Could have been." Henry's voice came quieter,
more distant.

"You don't look like a spook to me."

"You know one if you saw one?"
Ben opened his eyes, studied Henry's face. There was no
sarcasm in Henry's voice or eyes. Henry met his gaze.

"How'd you weave through all them gators? What
kept 'em away so long? How'd you know which way
to swim?"

"Stars. Instinct," the words sounded hollow as he
said them. "You have a lantern?"

Henry shook his head. "Things out here you can't
even guess at, Ben. I seen things I can't describe, much less
explain. Ain't nobody ever alone in the swamp." He smiled
at Ben's look. "I ain't crazy. We been through that." His
voice was low, with no hint of annoyance. "I may be the
sanest person around."

"Next to me," Ben laughed. His hallucination was
claiming sanity.

"No, you're nutty as a bedbug, Bubba. Off in your
own little world."

Ben tried to push himself up, but still didn't have the strength. He shook his head again. He was angry at a dream. "Whatever you say. '*Henry.*'"

"This is real, Ben. As real as Will and Daddy and that gator that bumped you. Maybe more so." Henry slapped Ben's cheek. "Ever dream anything that solid? I need to hurt you?"

Ben touched his cheek. This was Henry. Or a real person, anyway. And apart from the hair and beard, looking as young as ever. But how? "How could you be out here so long?"

"You're not listening again, Ben. I *been* all over. I come *back* here. And just in time. You and ol' Sammy been running wild, ain't you?"

"Sam, anyway."

"No sir. You're up to your teeth in it, Bubba, no matter what you tell yourself. I had a hell of a time straightening that out."

Something clicked in Ben's head then. "You broke into Sam's office."

"I did," Henry said. "Ol' Sam, he keeps records of everything. Always has. A weakness of his. Problem is, he keeps 'em well-hid."

"And I *did* see you in the crowd."

"Keeping an eye on you. Throwing roadblocks in front of you and Sammy."

"I stopped the fires!"

"Oh, but it's how you do a thing, ain't it, Ben,

not what or why. You looked your people in the eye and boldface lied."

"My people?"

"They trusted you. And you stuck a knife in their backs. Our backs. You got your due, and you know it," Henry's voice was harsher now, reverberating in the hollow space inside Ben.

"That was the only way to save... everything." The shame, the despair pulled at him as surely as the dark water had earlier.

"Ol' Super-Ben, flying in to save the day. Or your own hide." Henry leaned back, eyes narrowed. "That's the worrisome part – you believe your own crap. Only thing worse than a liar is a dishonest liar. That's the most dangerous person around."

"I did what I had to." Shame gave way to anger. Henry was baiting him. He had no idea what Ben had gone through. "I made the best of a bad situation – more than you ever did."

"You still don't get it, do you Bubba? You did what Sammy Archer wanted. Period. He stroked you 'til you purred, then got you to step in front of that 18-wheeler. And you thinking it was all for the best. Scapegoats aren't born, Ben, they're made. And ol' Sammy sure as hell made you." Ben shivered again, despite the fire and the blanket. Henry was talking like Kelly. Had he really been so blind? An ache inside, heavy as one of Will Jenkins' punches, told him Henry and Kelly were right. He wanted to yell that Henry was wrong, but he couldn't form the words.

Henry nodded. "How you think Will Jenkins got on you so fast? You ever known him to have an original thought? Or a quick one?"

"How do you know all that?"

"My business to know." Henry stared past Ben, eyes unfocused again. The stars over his shoulder hadn't moved. Ben started to speak, but Henry held up a hand. "Years back, Ben, your daddy wasn't the only one Sam Archer worked over. That Mangrove Underground crap felt like my idea... up until that business at the barge. Why'd all your daddy's schemes come crashing down like dominoes all of a sudden? Ol' Sammy played us all to get what he wanted.

"You never noticed how all the developers left, drug money disappeared, and the Park got expanded right after all that? That was 'for the good of Hermosa County,' too. Other folks went down, Sammy got his way and a promotion. And recruited a new whipping boy."

Ben shivered again. That was how Sam worked. And it fit with all that had happened in the past few days, in the past 10 years, since... his father. It was part of a pattern so big, so obvious, he should have seen it long ago. He had been too close, able to see small pieces, but not the entire picture. Sam's rants and pep talks had kept Ben distracted. Sam had ruined James Gates, then chosen Ben as the best tool at hand, one too angry at himself to see he was being used. He had been stupid. He was no better than his father. Ben tried to rise again, drag himself back to town to take down Sam Archer with his bare hands. He fell back, exhausted. Helpless. He had been right to have Kelly mail his account to Judge Barnes – that was the only way he had now of getting at Sam for... everything. And here was Henry Moton, smiling, saying he had been as wronged as Ben.

"So Sam walks away again?"

"Oh, Sammy's cooked." Henry grinned as big as Ben had ever seen. "Between that letter of yours and his records, he'll never see daylight again. If folks don't lynch him first."

It took a moment for Ben to realize what Henry had said. "You talked to Kelly!"

"She knows I'm around." He patted Ben's shoulder.

"And you sent that fax."

"Had to smoke ol' Sammy out, make him re-stash his papers and phone tapes." Henry patted a rucksack next to him. "Thinks he hid this stuff in the boondocks. Doesn't know the swamp has eyes."

"He actually kept records of all this?"

"Everything, Bubba. Everything. Including your part in it."

"So you saved my life so you could send me to jail? You should have just..."

"*Listen to me!*" Henry loomed over him. "I'm all you got going for you right now. And I'd as soon dump your lame ass. I don't need you. Nobody does. You're dead, Bubba, you just don't know it yet."

"So why'd you save me?"

"I owe you," Henry said softly.

"For..."

"The barge, Ben. You saved me back then. Couple times over. You pulled Kelly out, freed me up to grab your daddy. You let me run. You didn't cover for your daddy or try to hide what he done. You made my stupidity count for something."

"I covered my ass," Ben whispered. Self-loathing returned, as fresh as ever. "I betrayed my family. Doesn't matter who planned it. My dad died because of me."

"No, Ben. He died because of himself. That was his choice. You come through like a champ. Bravest sumbitch I know. Hung out yourself and everything you had to do right. 'Why' don't matter, remember? Anybody else would've nailed me, covered for his old man. I would have, if it'd been the other way around. 'Course, this place'd be a whole lot worse if you had."

"*You* climbed back in. *You* saved him. No one else would have done that." Ben's eyes felt hot, blurry. "Or could have." He turned his head and blinked to clear them.

"Ben, your daddy died in there, I'd've been up for murder." Henry's laugh rumbled deep again. "God's honest truth – I was scared of jail. And scooted for the brush quick as I could, you recall." Henry kicked at the fire. "A hero would have stayed, stood up for what he believed. Me, I wiggled down in a gator nest for fear of them night-vision scopes. Crawled in so deep I thought I'd never see daylight again."

"You're a hero to lots of people. Lots of Mangrove

Underground flags in town."

"Yeah, I seen 'em." Henry rolled his eyes. "People need lives."

"That means a lot."

"Does it?"

The nameless stars hung constant beyond the swaying branches. Since the night at the barge, he had envied Henry's commitment, Henry's bravery. For 10 years he had tried to live up to Henry's example, blaming any anger toward Henry on himself, on Kelly, fighting to justify his betrayal of his father, of Henry. He had ignored the festering self-hatred, idealizing Henry and hiding behind the ever-growing Henry Moton legend. Henry was a dead hero, and Ben carried on that legacy.

But now here was Henry, in person, crumbling that carefully-built reality with a word. Saying *he* respected *Ben*. The darkness surged up again, smothering him. Ben covered his ears to block out Henry's voice. Henry was working him, as surely as Sam Archer ever had. He focused on the stars beyond Henry's shoulders. They, at least, could be trusted.

"Tough to be beholden to someone you hate," Henry said.

"I don't..." Ben fell silent. How could he hate the man who saved his father, who proved himself a better man? It was so obvious: he hated Henry for being better, with James Gates, with Kelly. And now Henry was saying hate was OK. Ben hated him for that, too. Why would Henry help him? Ben wasn't worth it. He wasn't worth anything.

Long ago he had left Henry for dead. He wished Henry had left him in the dark water, where he could stop swimming and let the alligators take him.

Henry slapped Ben's arm, as if reading his thoughts. "Ben, back then you gave me something no one else ever had – a chance to start over. Intended or not, that was one hell of a gift. *That's* what I owe you. Pulling you out of that slough don't even come close to payback."

"You owe me nothing." Ben clenched his hands and teeth to keep the darkness in check.

Henry shook his head, a teacher seeking patience with a struggling student. "Listen. Right now you got nothing. That's not all bad. It means you got nothing to lose." Henry smiled at Ben's confusion. "By now, folks think you're dead. I'm giving you the same gift you gave me. Up to you what you do with it."

"I'm crap," Ben whispered to the stars.

"Well, crap makes the best fertilizer, Bubba." Henry's rumbling laugh filled the small clearing. "Thing is, you got options. A chance to see what you can grow."

"What options?" Not that it mattered. He was too drained to argue, anyway. Henry was as crazy as ever, but his talk of hope pushed the darkness back ever so slightly.

Henry grinned again and scooted closer. "One – you can disappear. Start fresh as someone else. You got a good start on that. I can help you there, set you up with friends. Belize, then Cuba, and that's the last anyone knows of you. How's your Spanish?"

205

"Non-existent."

"Uh huh. Two – you can stay in-country. I might could help with that, too. They may find you someday, but at least you speak the language."

"They haven't found you."

"This ain't about me."

"Three... I stay here and help you?"

"Lord, no. I told you, I don't want you. No, you could go back. Face 'em down. Come clean." Henry paused, studying Ben. "Face yourself down, too. See if you couldn't whup some inner demons." Henry paused again. The smile faded. "That probably means jail, though. If Will Jenkins and Daddy don't get you first."

Ben closed his eyes. Running and hiding was the obvious choice, especially if Henry would help. There was nothing for him in Hermosa County. What could he do against Sam Archer? Against the entire community? He was furious at Sam, but Henry was right – Sam wasn't the enemy, Ben himself was. In another place, another country, he could start fresh, be someone else, build something worthwhile.

Ben opened his eyes. Henry's face floated in front of him. Ben had turned his back on people he loved before. How could he think of doing that again, with Henry a reminder of everything Ben could have been. Ben knew what he should do, but even Henry listed running as the first option.

They had left him for dead once. Next time they'd make sure, long before he could get anywhere near Archer. Ben thought of Sam's talk about bureaucrats manufacturing evidence against him. By now Sam would have painted Ben's name so black... Henry was still watching him. He didn't trust Henry, or his talk of destroying Sam. Or that Henry was real. But the hope of a fresh start was a beacon in the darkness.

"You really went to Cuba?"

"*Si, compañero,*" Henry laughed. "For a bit, anyway."

"I... what should I do?" He hated the weakness that made him ask the question.

"Oh, no. Advice is dangerous, Ben. Cuts both ways. I don't mind helping. I'll even bankroll your start-up. But I can't make choices for you. You know what's right. And it's got nothing to do with me."

"Maybe." He could learn Spanish. He could learn anything. But his duty was in Cypress City. But where best to shake free of this self-loathing?

"No hurry," Henry said. "Relax here. Get your strength. I'll drop you back in the real world, wherever you want, whenever you're ready. Meantime, I got some stew going you might be interested in."

Only then did Ben smell the food cooking. His mouth watered, and his stomach grumbled. He hadn't eaten for more than a day.

Henry helped Ben sit up, then handed him a wooden bowl filled with stew. Ben spooned broth and vegetables into his mouth. The stew tasted musty, vaguely familiar yet totally foreign at the same time. A warmth spread through him as he ate. His muscles relaxed. His eyelids drooped. He forced them open and took a second helping from Henry.

"What is this?" Ben poked at the stew with his spoon.

"What you need, Bubba. Good for what ails you."

"I can barely keep my eyes open."

"That's not a bad thing, either. Ain't nothing can mess with you here."

"Sounds like I should stay here." His voice sounded fuzzy, slurred.

"Hiding ain't the answer. You got to do something eventually."

"What do you want me to do?"

"Uh uh, sneaky coyote. I will tell you this, though: you go back to town, or anywhere else, thinking like you do now, you won't last a day. There's you, and there's the rest of the world. You need to seriously rethink that relationship."

"Maybe if you gave more advice you'd be better at it." Ben lay back and set the bowl on his stomach. "Cuba's nice?"

"Beautiful, Bubba. So bright and green and beautiful you about cry just looking at it."

The words came softer, quieter. Ben tried to keep his eyes open, but Henry's face grew fainter with his voice. The campfire dimmed and the unmoving stars faded.

## 20

*In the barge that night, the smoke, the heat, the groaning bulkheads all fell away. All I could see was Ben's face – lit for a moment by a flare outside – watching me, stunned. Then it went cold, less... human... than I'd ever seen.*

*He saw me. Us.*

*I wasn't tied up. Or trying to get away.*

(He saw me kiss Henry.)

*His eyes filled with something I'd never seen there. Something dark. Then the flare faded, and the smoke swirled between us again.*

*Henry and I were through by then – I was there that night to settle all that. Then Ben dropped through the hatch. It wasn't supposed to happen. Not like that. Like I'd punched him. Like he'd punched me.*

(He saw me kiss Henry.)

*Then boots pounded on the metal above us. I heard Ben turn back toward the ladder, hands scraping rust as he felt his way along the bulkhead. I heard Henry behind me, cutting the duct tape off Mr. Gates' wrists and ankles.*

Then something flashed, lifted me, and threw me back down. My eyes stung. Plywood mashed into my cheek. My lungs were coming up, but I couldn't hear myself cough. All I could do was lay there. Something bumped my foot, and then I was hanging head-down, bouncing.

I knew Ben's shoulders, his back. Their feel, their smell. Reassuring. Then terrifying. I wasn't scared of him. I hated myself at that moment. What he'd seen...

I don't know why he came back. I wouldn't have. It was an adventure – the fling with Henry, his crazy plans, all of it. Intense. Exciting the way he explained it – strike a blow for the common man, free the Park land for the people. Upstaging the mermaid show would be a laugh, he said. A way for me to kiss SafariLand good-bye in style.

I didn't know he'd make it look like a kidnapping. I didn't know he'd grabbed Mr. Gates, either. I didn't know he was that crazy.

I had him talked down, though. Seeing sense. Ready to take Mr. Gates and me back to town.

Then came the yelling and explosions outside, all the smoke pouring in. And Ben dropping out of the sky to save me.

I loved Ben. For him to have seen...

(He saw me kiss Henry.)

I don't think Ben knew why he came back for me. Ever. I'd crushed him, but something – love, guilt, loyalty – 'strong care attachment,' he called it later – was still there. He just reacted, I guess. 'Care' was stronger than anything *else. Forced himself back in to find me. And me wishing he would drop me, leave me there to die. Instead, he carried me up the ladder, into fresh air and safety.*

*Then there were guns and faces shouting silently and hands pulling me from him, lowering me down the barge. I barely saw anything through the tears. I wanted to crawl back in, never see the hatred on his face again.*

*Then, from across the clearing, we watched fire explode through the hatches. Camp fuel on plywood flooring, explosives, they never knew what, sent flames tearing through the canvas-and-frond covers. Deputies ran from the barge, like cartoon people running across a movie screen. A deputy put a hand on my shoulder, holding me there.*

*Beside me, Ben watched the flames, too, face like cold iron. He looked down at me, from miles away, as if searching for someone he knew.*

(He saw me kiss Henry.)

*"Your dad's OK, right?" I said. My voice echoed in my head. I knew Henry'd be fine, but I hadn't seen Mr. Gates since we'd climbed out.*

*Ben just stared, like I'd spoken Greek. I looked around. Mr. Gates was nowhere. That's when I realized Ben had no idea his dad was in the barge, or that Henry had kidnapped him. He had charged in to save me, nothing more. I yelled, trying to get him to understand. He didn't budge. Deputies heard me, though, and ran back to the barge. I saw it click in Ben's eyes, but he still didn't move. He just... didn't. Like he didn't care.*

*Or he cared too much.*

*He had to have known, or suspected, what his dad had been doing. How could he not? He would have hated that, hated being linked to that. Despised his dad for it.*

*Then to see me and Henry... It was too much all at once. Everyone close to him had betrayed him. To him, we all deserved to burn.*

(He saw me kiss Henry.)

*Ben shut his eyes. I slapped him, hard, and yelled as loud as I could. The ring he'd just given me left a cut on his cheek. I tried to run back, but the deputy had me tight.*

*Ben finally stepped toward the barge. But dragging his feet just enough so two deputies could grab him, hold him back. It looked like Ben, but he was someone else, doing something Ben would never do.*

*That's when Henry climbed out, silhouetted against the flames, Mr. Gates limp across his shoulders. He was dressed in SWAT fatigues, like the rest of them, but it was Henry. The set of the shoulders, the broad stance gave him away. And only Henry would have run back into a fire to save an enemy.*

*I looked at Ben, then quickly away. In that instant, I'd never hated anyone so much as I hated him. It should have been him, not Henry. Ben hesitating, it was like he'd left me to burn. Like I'd never known him.*

*"Bravest thing I've ever seen," the deputy beside me mouthed.*

*"You have no idea," I said.*

Ben dropped to his knees at that, like he'd been shot. He grabbed at me, but I pulled away. Henry handed Mr. Gates to the deputies, then ran into the bushes.

Something cold and thick slid between Ben and me then. Shoulder-to-shoulder, we had never been so far apart. He knelt in the dirt, shaking. I wanted to kick him. God help me, but I did. To break down when he could have done something... To leave his dad to die... Henry was crazy, but that night Ben was beyond vile.

Then Sammy Archer was there, arm around Ben's shoulders, shaking him, telling him he'd done fine, just fine. "Welcome to the team, Ben," he said when the deputies chased after Henry. "You've thrown in with the good guys. Remember that." I remember it, word-for-word, though it didn't make sense until later. Sammy was behind everything. But how could I tell Ben that, ever?

After, Sammy led us to the Park boat. Deputies carried Mr. Gates in the sheriff's office launch behind us. No one spoke as we idled away, each staring away from the fires, into the mangrove darkness crowding close.

Ben was a zombie for the ride back. He had to have been angry, scared, guilty, relieved all at once. Or maybe that was just me. My best friend was sitting next to me, but I didn't know him. We rode like that for hours, forever, no sense of time or space, only the hollow ache and the outboard's hum.

At the first hint of town lights, he finally spoke.

"Kel?" His voice barely sounded above the engine.

*"You could have saved him."* It was all I could say.

*"You could have told me."* His voice was louder.

*"He might have died."* I couldn't look at him. *"You could save me, but you're your father?"* If his dad had died and I'd lived... I couldn't have lived with myself.

*"Who put him there?"* I'd never heard his voice so ugly.

I slapped his head sideways then. He stared at me, hating me right back, but unable to say it. Or unwilling to, knowing he had himself to hate as well.

It was all there in his eyes, all the pieces dropping into place. Despising himself for not seeing it before. I had shoved a knife into him, but he had twisted it, done more damage than I could ever do. He couldn't face that. Not then, anyway. He sat there, glaring death, angrier at me than he had any right to be.

*"You're not who I thought you were,"* I said.

*"At least I'm honest,"* he said.

He believed that. And always would, no matter what else he did. He could convince himself anything he did was for the highest purpose, all the while ignoring everything that screamed otherwise. It's what finally tripped him up with Sammy.

I took the ring off, set it on his knee. He held it for a moment, then dropped it overboard. We both sat stunned then. The dark water sluiced by. Things weren't supposed to happen like that, not between us. They just weren't.

Later, with the investigators, he said nothing about

214

me and Henry. Or his dad. I don't know why he put himself at risk like that. 'Strong care attachment,' I guess. And enough people – like Sammy – knew the truth that he could have gone to jail for a while.

An attempt at atonement, maybe. Ben's moment of truth had come, and he'd failed. Or worse, failed to act. Henry saved his dad when he couldn't. Then Ben betrayed himself. He couldn't face the things in him he despised most, the things he'd never have words for. Or the courage to admit, even to himself:

Shame that he hadn't acted.

Anger that I knew.

Fear that someone else might find out.

## 21

Ben woke to warmth on his face and a soft glow in his eyes. The sun, through low clouds or fog. The muddy smell of sawgrass flats clung so thick he could taste it. Silence. The fog, or mist, cloaked everything in shades of gray. At his feet, crushed limerock stretched 20 yards to a line of crumbling asphalt. Two gasoline pumps on a cement pad loomed dark a quarter of the way to the road.

Ben rolled his head, feeling his neck bones crackle. He sat on a wooden bench, head back against the plate glass window of a low, cypress-paneled building. He turned enough to read 'Swamp Man's Cafe and Gifts' in gold letters on the glass. No lights showed inside.

Ben closed his eyes, searching for a memory of the place. No, it was new to him. He tried to remember getting there, but couldn't recall anything since chasing Sam Archer... however long ago it had been. He had stopped at the stilt house, then Will Jenkins had been there. The skiff, the dark water rushed back. And Henry Moton. The ground tilted. He clutched his ribs and winced. The beating, at least, had been real. He must have reached shore, dragged himself here. His clothes, though, were clean, and unfamiliar – canvas pants, denim shirt, green fatigue jacket. Only his boots were his. And the familiar outline of the Silva compass in his shirt pocket. He had borrowed clothes, then. Or stolen them.

A low growl sounded in the fog. Tires rushing along asphalt. He squinted, anxious about who might be coming. The mist rippled, glowed with twin headlights, and a black Suburban materialized, Spanish moss streaming from its antenna. Ben caught a glimpse of a cocker spaniel sitting in a woman's lap, head out the window, ears and tongue flapping. Two freckled children leaned out the backseat window, wind whipping their hair.

"Swamp Maaaan!" the little girl yelled as her brother screeched "Ba-ha-haaaa!" Then the fog closed behind them, and they were gone as quickly as they had come. Ben sat still, listening to the tires recede. He touched his ribs, winced. He wasn't dreaming. It was good to be sure of that much.

The fog brightened. The gas pumps grew more distinct. He heard the lower-pitched hum of car tires, traveling slowly. Headlights appeared, then a small sedan, nearly white with dust. The car slowed, turned into the limerock parking lot and stopped 20 feet to Ben's right. The driver, a woman in her thirties maybe, with her hair pulled back, let the engine run as she stared at Ben. After a moment she rolled down the window several inches.

"I help you?" she yelled.

"It okay to sit for a bit?" Ben yelled back.

"We ain't open yet," she yelled. "You waiting for someone?"

"Not that I know of."

"What are you doing here?"

"Wondering where 'here' is." Ben hoped he sounded non-threatening.

The woman hesitated, then yelled, "Well, I gotta open up. You need to get."

Ben looked around him. "To where?"

"Wherever you came from."

"Lady, if I knew where that was I'd be there." He ached at the idea of getting up, much less walking.

The woman chewed her lip, eyes darting from Ben's face to his clothes, then around the parking lot. She turned off the engine. "You sit right there. Don't move."

"Done."

"I got a gun," she yelled.

"I don't doubt that."

The woman held up a small revolver.

Ben raised his hands. After his run-in with Will Jenkins and Delmore Moton, this woman and her gun didn't seem threatening. All he had to do was sit still.

The woman stepped from her car and crossed to the restaurant. Bells jangled as she opened the door, slipped inside, and slammed the deadbolt back in place.

Ben leaned back, not sure what to do next. The

woman was probably calling the police. He could wait for them, tell them... what? What would they do? Arrest him for loitering? Send him back to Cypress City? He should run. But to where? Or if there were a phone inside he could call... Kelly? He didn't want to drag her any deeper in this, have Delmore Moton, or Sam, to go after her, too. He could start walking, hitch a ride home. He should have asked the woman which direction Cypress City was.

The fog thinned. A white van pulled into the gravel lot and stopped in front of him. A man jumped out, bundle of newspapers under one arm. He nodded to Ben, dropped a loose paper at the restaurant door, then keyed open a Miami Herald box and slid the rest of the papers inside.

"You wouldn't be going to town, would you?" Ben asked.

"What town?" The man scowled and drove away. Ben leaned forward, chin in his hands. His face felt prickly. The stubble was thick as a three-day growth. No wonder people were keeping their distance. How long had he been gone? He picked up the newspaper from the ground beside him. Wednesday, the 18th. Will had grabbed him Saturday morning. But he had no memory of those days, only a dream about meeting Henry Moton.

Ben thumbed through the paper. In the *State* section, he found a brief story about state and local authorities looking for a Hermosa County man wanted for arson and manslaughter. Ben's throat tightened. His hands and legs felt numb. Sam had burned him good. He recalled his dream-conversation with Henry. Something inside him had known this would happen. He couldn't go back to Cypress City. Or call Kelly. They'd be listening to her phone.

The café door swung open with a jangle of keys and hanging bells.

"Hey, you OK?" The woman leaned out the door. "You look a little rattled."

"Rattled doesn't scratch the surface."

"Look, there's no food yet 'cause asshole Bert is late again, but I got some coffee on."

"Thanks," Ben whispered. He didn't have the strength to run, and the cops would be there soon. Judge Barnes should have his letter by now. That would work in his favor. He could at least have coffee while he waited. Ben dug his hands into empty pants pockets. "I don't know if I have any..." But the woman had stepped inside.

Ben reached into a jacket pocket, was surprised to feel a small bundle. He pulled out a red cloth folded around something flat, square. Inside the bandana-sized cloth was a stack of $50 bills, folded over once and held together with a red rubber band. He thumbed trough the bills, counting $2,000. A piece of yellow legal paper was tucked under the rubber band as well. Ben unfolded it. On one side were names and addresses in Belize City and Havana. 'Your Call' was scribbled at the bottom. On the other side were names and addresses in Maine and Saskatchewan. Ben's hands shook. He knew the handwriting, though he hadn't seen it for years. He spread the bandana on his knees, knowing what he would see: a magic-markered broccoli silhouette with a long tangle of roots beneath it.

The ground tilted again. Every detail of Henry's campsite rushed back, as sharp as if Ben were still there. Had he been there three, four days? The bandana, the money were solid in his hands. They could have come from nowhere else. Ben pushed hard on his ribs until he yelped. This was real. Henry had dropped him here. Somewhere south, if he was reading *The Herald*. But how far south? And the money... Henry's, "I'll even bankroll you..." sprang to mind. Henry was pushing him. Toward Cuba. Or was he simply making the choice easier for Ben – making a jump in any direction as simple as possible?

The woman was watching through the plate glass window, arms folded. He smiled at her, stuffed the money and bandana in his pocket and stepped to the door.

Inside the diner was dim, lit only by strings of small white holiday lights running along low wooden rafters. Old license plates covered the cedar-paneled walls. An assortment from Texas hung to his left. Aruba and Mexico were nailed on the side of the counter in front of him. Cuba hung above the kitchen door. Ben nodded a 'thank you' to the woman and slid into a booth by the window. A red-and-white Wyoming license plate hung from the wall beside him. The white fairy lights flashed around the window's edge. A neon 'Open' sign crackled to life by the door. The opening strains of Vivaldi's 'Spring' came soft from overhead.

Outside, patches of fog eddied across the road as the sun warmed the asphalt. Why had Henry left him so far from Cypress City? He pulled out Henry's note again. He should call Henry's friends? He saw again the arching branches, the firelight, and the intensity of Henry's eyes. No. It was his call what to do next.

A coffee mug thunked on the table in front of him. The woman stood back from the booth, hands on her hips.

"No gun?" Ben asked.

"You're not trouble," she shook her head. "Not sure what you are, but it's not that."

Ben sipped the coffee. "You sound pretty sure."

"You look rode hard and left out, but not like that's a natural condition." She studied him for a moment. "Who dumped you off?"

"Why 'dumped?'" Was she one of Henry's friends? "No car. And no place to walk from." She pulled a plastic nametag from her pocket and pinned it on her blouse. 'Suzanne.'

"So when do the cops get here?"

"Cops? Oh." Suzanne waved a hand. The gesture slid an invisible weight from Ben's shoulders. "Like I said, you're not trouble. In trouble, maybe, but not dangerous."

"Except to myself."

She watched him sip his coffee. "You sure you're OK?"

"Just trying to figure things out. Like where I am." Suzanne nodded toward the roadway. "Tamiami Trail. U.S.

41? Miami's 30-some miles that way." She pointed in the direction the newspaper van had gone. "Where you from?"

"I... uuh, Tampa."

"Well, you're a lifetime from Tampa." She studied him for a moment. "And not too concerned about that. Know your name?"

"Ben. Ben... uuh, Jenkins."

Suzanne leaned back against the counter, fighting a smile. "Don't seem like amnesia, Ben uuh-Jenkins from uuh-Tampa."

"Yeah. But the only person who knows I'm here, or cares, is the one who dropped me off. And I'm not even sure he exists. That doesn't make sense, but it's all I've got. Thanks for the coffee. And for not shooting me. I'll be gone as soon as I find a ride."

The bells over the door jangled. Three men walked in, identical except for their faded flannel shirts and straw cowboy hats. All had the same weathered faces of years in the sun.

"Hey, Suzie-Q!" The first man said. The other two men smiled at Suzanne and nodded toward Ben. "Still got that longhair music going?"

"Bert's idea, Vernon. Says it keeps out the riff-raff. Y'all keep coming back, though." She patted Ben's arm. "I'll be right back." She stepped behind the counter. "Nothing but coffee, fellas. His lordship hasn't seen fit to grace us yet." Suzanne poured coffee then went to the kitchen.

The men talked quietly, heads close, ignoring Ben. Out the window, the fog was still rising. He could go anywhere. Henry had seen to that. Ben fingered the Mangrove Underground bandana. He could pull a Henry, go back, grab Sam, force a confession. His stomach clenched at that, though. He wouldn't repeat that ugly bit of family history. If he could even pull it off. He couldn't even get out of town without getting beat up. How could he hope to get back in, abduct an on-guard Sam Archer, and get away again?

Ben spread the bandana on the table, smoothed it out with both hands. His duty was in Hermosa County, but he couldn't simply go back. He could call Judge Barnes, but that would mean completely trusting the man who had destroyed his father. Even with Kelly on his side, could he ever get a fair hearing there? He ran a finger over the red cloth, tracing the outline of the mangrove roots. He envied Henry the ability to see the right choice and immediately take action.

There was no way to get at Sam without destroying himself. And the community. Or what passed for a community. Sam was tied to the place more closely than Ben had ever been. Ben was expendable. And it sounded like Henry would take care of Archer himself. Ben squeezed his coffee mug to keep a fist from forming.

'Rethink your relationship with the world ,' Henry had said. Ben didn't know where to start. He felt as if he were floating, drifting with the fog outside. He stuffed the bandana in his pocket. The yellow paper fell to the table. 'Your Call' screamed up at him.

"We got food, mystery man." Suzanne dropped a menu in front of him. "And I might have a ride back north, if you're interested." Ben barely felt her hand on his arm. "I was thinking south might be better." His voice sounded as distant as hers. This wasn't right. It wasn't him. He didn't run away. Or did he? He had been running away all his life. But here, now, he saw no other way.

Suzanne nodded. "Yeah, it might be." She squeezed his shoulder. "Anyplace specific or just 'south'?"

Ben slid the paper from beneath the menu. He could have been talking to himself, or imagining Suzanne's responses. "Anyplace'll do. It's..." Ben glanced up at the woman's brown eyes. "Suzanne, you ever have a second chance at something? A totally fresh start, a clean slate?"

"You got that now?"

Ben shrugged.

"Most people'd kill for that," Suzanne said.

"Yeah." Ben stared at the menu. The future hung in front of him, pale and shifting. Any direction he picked would be the right one. And the wrong one. Seconds, minutes passed.

"Hey." Suzanne's voice echoed from far away. "You got a place to stay, anywhere to go?"

Ben shook his head without looking up.

"Gimme a second. Vernon's always looking for people to

work up by Okeechobee. Picking peppers, right now. But it's room and board, if you don't mind picking peppers..." Warmth spread through him. "Picking peppers sounds just fine."

Suzanne squeezed his shoulder and walked back to the three men sitting at the counter.

The flatbed truck bounced along the raised roadway, cane fields spreading as far as

Ben could see. The dozen men riding in the back squatted as near the truck's cab as possible, caps and up-turned collars hiding their faces. Ben crouched at the rear of the group, ducking as low out of the wind as he could. The last of the morning fog had burned off, but the air was still cool and damp. He stared past his knees, where the truck bed's wooden slats shifted with every bump and pothole. He felt the other men watching him with sidelong glances, dark eyes taking in every feature of his death-pale face, his mis-matched clothes, his office-soft hands. The truck bounced. Ben grabbed at a wooden side rail to keep his balance. Men reached to steady each other. No one reached to Ben. That was fine. He hadn't realized how much he would stand out in a group of farm workers. People looking and dressing like him didn't just climb on work trucks at roadside restaurants, with the farm owner slapping them on the back.

Ben grinned despite the chill wind and his unease. He was a total stranger for the first time in his life. Here on the truck no one knew him, his family, or their generations of history. He was drifting, rootless, alone. Ben knew he should be frightened, but he felt free in a way he had never felt before. He was something new, at the edge of something new to him, with no idea what would happen next.

The men had nodded, eyes guarded, when he climbed aboard at Swamp Man's.

Vernon had called out something in Spanish, and they had shuffled aside to make room for him without making eye contact. Ben had nodded thanks and squatted at the edge of the group. He had spent the time since trying to understand the Spanish the men whispered to each other, but could make no sense of it. Ben had smiled to himself. This was perfect. He needed to learn the language quickly. He would immerse himself with these men.

Then had come the constant stops as the truck picked up new workers or dropped off others. The newcomers would edge past Ben to sit forward. Ben smiled and nodded, trying to look friendly. No one spoke to him or looked directly at him. They had to think he was a farm-owner's spy. Or INS. Ben settled on watching the dusty floorboards, hoping newcomers at each stop would be more friendly. They would reach the pepper fields soon, anyway. He would work with them, gain their trust over time. He shuffled toward the truck cab, out of the wind.

"*¡O! ¡Quita de allá!*" The voice was loud and the words distinct, though Ben didn't understand them. One of the men stood in front of him, hand on another's shoulder, glaring down. Ben smiled, shook his head.

"*¡Quita de allá! ¡Mi amigo quiere sentarse allá!*" The man waved his hand toward the rear of the truck, back the way they had come.

227

*"No. No. Esta bien."* The other man shook the hand from his shoulder and inched away. Others whispered, hissed at the man confronting Ben.

*"Uhh... no entiendo..."* Ben glanced toward the whisperers, inviting one of them to translate. If he didn't take offense, one of the others might step in to defuse things. One of the older men spoke in Spanish. He and Ben's antagonist glared at each other. After several moments of silence, the first man stepped away but kept unblinking eyes on Ben.

Ben smiled, as if at a joke among friends. The man might not have been starting a fight. He could have been testing Ben's Spanish, seeing how Ben would react. It didn't matter. Despite the tension on the truck, Ben felt relaxed for the first time since... he couldn't remember when. This was the beginning of something he didn't understand, but that was nonetheless drawing him on, unfolding around him as he watched. There on the back of the farm truck, morning air swirling cool over him, he felt reborn. Or about to be. He had no desire beyond sitting, watching the floorboards bounce, and feeling the wind rush past. There was peace enough in that for a lifetime.

The truck slowed then stopped. The driver yelled something in Spanish, and the men all piled off to join a larger group of men and women already in the pepper fields. Feeling light, as if he were floating, Ben stepped off with them.

*"¡No, pendejo! ¡Permanece en el camion!* The man who had confronted him stood in his way.

228

Ben shook his head, smiled.

"*¡Nadie te quieren aquí!  ¿Me entiendo?*" The man leaned closer, put a hand on Ben's chest.

Ben looked for the old man who had stepped in before.  He was gone.  Ben heard the truck drop into gear and pull away behind him.  He raised his hands and shook his head again.

"*No entiendo.  No... comprendo.*"  Ben stepped around the man, down the slope to the roadside field.  Workers parted to let him pass.  A hand fell on his shoulder, spun Ben around.

"*¿Entiendas esta?*"  The blade flashed bright between them.

Ben stepped back, arms wide.  He felt the people around him back away, heard them yelling, smelled the fresh-turned earth of the field.  The man stepped toward him, knife sweeping past Ben's face.  Ben jumped back again, as if watching the scene from the crowd of workers.  He moved in slow motion, as slow as the knife gliding past.  The feeling he had on the truck swept through him again, stronger now.  He was part of a process pulling him on, defining him, remaking him.  He had no power to change what was happening.  He didn't want to die, but neither wants nor desires had a place here.  He was playing a part in a larger pattern he could only guess at.  And if it all ended here, now, in violence, that was alright.  He was awe-struck by the beauty of the morning sunlight glinting off the polished blade, the exact line the man's arm traced as it slashed past

Ben's midsection. He marveled at the sharp arc sweeping forward, a curved rail, to intersect the line of his stomach long before the knife moved. He watched, fascinated as the blade slid along that arc even as his body arched away from it.

"It's okay," he heard his voice say from somewhere far away. "You can't hurt me." He smiled. The man wasn't his enemy. He was simply playing a role, as caught up in this as Ben. The man paused, as if not believing what he saw or heard. The people around them stood frozen, silent, looking at Ben with the same disbelief. The scene hung suspended, in a breath-held balance, waiting for some movement to set it in motion again.

Ben stepped toward the man, hands wide, ready to dodge aside, but not concerned if he didn't. Fear played across the man's face, then hatred. Then several things happened at once.

The man lunged. Ben jumped back, felt a burning along his midsection. Three men leaped at the attacker, pulled him back before he came close to Ben, and wrestled the knife away. The rest of the crowd backed off, some crossing themselves as they stared from Ben's face, to his torso, and back to his face.

Ben rubbed a hand across his burning stomach and was surprised to feel wetness, as if the scuffle had made him sweat. Looking down, he saw his hand smeared with red, and a darker stain across the front of his sliced-open shirt. Ben watched, detached, feeling nothing more than a slight burning, as the stain spread downward. He touched his stomach again, felt a finger slip between a gash of skin and muscle. The cut, from one side of his ribs, across his stomach to the opposite ribs, stung at his touch, but nothing more. Not yet. The blood seeped to his waistband. Ben took off his jacket, rolled it up and pressed it to his stomach to stop the bleeding.

Four men held his attacker to the ground. They and the others watched Ben, waiting for him to speak, move, react. Ben looked past the people and across the fields. Sunlight lit the pepper plants from behind, turning their leaves into fragments of green stained glass. The muddy smell of the fields filled him, so similar to the tidal mud he knew, yet subtly different, less wild, but no less fertile. Two dozen faces, warm in the sunlight, stared at him, expectantly. He started to speak, but could think of no words to compare with the scene.

He had wanted to join these people, work with them, live with them, help them. That had been a foolish hope. Ben was as far apart from them as he had been apart from the people in Hermosa County. Or as he had kept himself apart, he realized. Despite all his efforts, all his posturing and delusions of heroism, he had kept them at a distance. Even Kelly. He had never really helped the town or any of the people he had called his own. He had only helped himself. No, he had even screwed that up. All his life Kelly, the people in Cypress City, had known what he only now realized.

His attacker still glared at him. Ben smiled at him and shook his head. The man was ignorant, scared, acting no different than Ben had acted all his life. Ben couldn't save the world. He couldn't even salvage this small confrontation. The newness, the language barrier that had seemed so promising an hour before now glared back at him and burned across his gut. He didn't belong here. He never would. And if he couldn't find refuge here, what chance did he have in Belize or Havana?

Ben pressed the jacket tighter. Feeling strangely weak, he dropped to his knees in the soft earth, overwhelmed by the beauty around him, with this brush of violence, and something else he didn't quite understand. The men and women rushed to him then. Supporting hands slipped around his shoulders and across his back. Distant voices urged him to lie back, relax, breathe slowly. Faces pressed close, concerned, speaking other words he didn't understand. One man put a hand over Ben's hands and began reciting something in Spanish.

"It's OK. I'm OK." He put a reddened hand on the man's shoulder. "Save prayers for someone in trouble." The man stared at him, wide-eyed.

"You *do* speak Spanish," a woman said.

"No," Ben said, "but I understand."

These were good people, but they weren't his people. He could only burden them. Like he had burdened the people of Cypress City. Starting over here, or anywhere else, was a fool's dream. He saw himself at the end of a long, frayed string of actions. If the scene had hung in an unseen balance moments before, surely he did, too. Henry had been wrong – there were not unlimited choices spread before him, as much as he wanted to believe that. The only choice was whether to accept his only possible action, as certain as the bright blade tracing its arc across his midsection before moving on to its logical, precise end. He would do this one thing right, wherever it took him. He gripped the praying man's shoulder tighter and pulled himself to his feet.

"You're hurt!" The woman who had spoken before slid an arm around him, steering him back.

"No. Not much." Ben eased her hands away. "It doesn't matter." He turned from the crowd, smiled at his attacker, still pinned to the ground. The man spat at him. Ben pressed the jacket tighter and walked from the field. He climbed to the raised roadway and began the long walk back down the asphalt toward the main highway.

## 22

*OK then, Brian Portis thought, civilization couldn't be too far away.  If his directions were good.  The high, bright valleys of that morning had given way to early darkness, thickening snowfall and this low, winding road along the river.  An unseasonable front rolling through, catching him off-guard and leaving the countryside deserted.  But that was OK.*

*Idaho Falls was around-the-next-bend close.  If he hadn't missed a turn.  Or made a wrong one.  He switched off the CD player.  Robert Earl Keen had been stuck in the damn thing for two days.  Portis had been singing along with it since Laramie, keeping himself distracted with songs of Texas, songs of home.  Distracted with thoughts of a different life.  Too distracted, maybe.*

*It had been hours since he had seen another car or anything resembling a town.  Swan Valley had been a wide spot on the ass of nowhere, and Jackson was two icy passes ago, with snow falling all the way.  Landmarks, any sense of* direction were lost in this landscape of gray land and sky. But it was OK.

He blew on his hands again, rubbed them together for warmth. The in-dash heater had stopped working hours before, though that had seemed a minor inconvenience at first. Now, in the gloom and snow, Portis cursed at it. The rented convertible that had seemed the bright spot in this God-forsaken sales trip was slowly turning him into a popsicle.

The canvas roof flapped loud over his head in a fresh gust that sent the car fishtailing. OK, then. The slush on the road was freezing. For the umpteenth time that day, Brian Portis wished he were back in Corpus Christi, back in his old office, back with Sally and the kids.

The road ahead seemed darker, dark as the land to either side. He flipped the headlight switch twice, three times. The dash lights winked on-and-off, but the road remained dark. Perfect. Just perfect. First the heater, now the lights. Avis would get a hot letter about this one.

Portis eased to a stop on the deserted highway and stepped out to check the headlights. Frost crunched under his wingtips with every step. The grill was a snow-bank suspended a foot above the road, the recessed head-lights glowing dim through inches of accumulated snow. He scraped the snow away and nodded at the beams lighting the snow-covered roadway ahead. He kicked as much snow as he could from the radiator as well, hoping that would fix the heater.

*Back behind the wheel, Portis held his hands to the heat vents. Nothing. OK then. The fan was broken. Or frozen. He slapped his hands on his thighs, trying to warm them. Idaho Falls was close. He could warm up there, get some coffee, then make the hour run to Pocatello on a proper interstate. A sales call tomorrow, then two more in Salt Lake, and he could turn in this damned car and fly back to sun and warmth and family and what was left of his life.*

*Brian Portis eased the car down what looked like the roadway. Trees lined either side of a flat, open stretch of snow like dark guideposts, but there were gaps where the road might curve, fork or twist just about anywhere.*

*He should have been in town hours ago. Had he missed a sign? What he remembered of the map showed a straight shot into the town, but there could be turns the map hadn't shown. The map, of course, that had blown out of his hands and across the wheat fields outside Victor. Like the heater, that had seemed a minor inconvenience.*

*The car swayed again, and Portis coaxed it back to where he thought the roadway should be. Everything still felt level beneath the tires, so that was good. Even if he was lost, if he kept moving he would eventually reach somewhere. Get directions. Not that stopping out here was an option, anyway.*

*Snow fell harder and in thick, wet clumps. He squinted into the deepening gloom. The headlights were clogging again. Once more he stopped, scraped them clear, letting his hands linger on the warm lights. Slush seeped over his ankles, filling his shoes with icy water.*

Back in the car, a red light flashed on the console. The gas gauge. Idiot, he thought. He should have stopped for gas in Swan Valley. But he had been singing. And dreaming of warmth. Idaho Falls had seemed... there. Oh, well. He would go as far as he could, keep an eye out for houses, buildings, anything. He wiggled his toes to keep them warm. If he could just find a road sign, anything, to tell him he was on the right track. The wind sent snow snakes swirling down the road ahead of him.

Something dark loomed on the roadside. A highway sign, maybe. His tires crunched on the freezing road. So dark – his headlights must be clogging again. He squinted through the windshield. It wasn't a road sign. A post, maybe. But a moving post. A person?

He knew people out here prided themselves on being hardy, but to be walking in weather like this? Whoever it was was probably lost, too. And freezing. Portis slowed. The figure turned to face him. A man, bundled and hunched, carrying a bag or small pack pressed against his stomach. He held out a hand, signaling Portis to stop.

This is crazy, Brian Portis thought: stopping for a stranger in the middle of nowhere. What choice did he have, though? The man looked hurt. And he might know the way to town. Or the closest gas station. Besides, here, out west, stopping for strangers seemed somehow OK. He stopped and rolled down the passenger window.

"You OK?" Portis yelled.

"Yeah. Sure." The stranger yelled back to be heard

*above the wind.* "*But a break from this crap would be nice.*"
*The man squinted for a good look at Portis, snow clinging to
a scraggly beard.*

*Portis hesitated, then opened the door. The man
slipped inside, wincing and clutching his midsection as
he did.*

"*You sure you're alright?*"

"*Old injury acting up. Cold weather's a killer, you
know?*" *He shook snow from his jacket and daypack, then
shut the door.* "*Thanks. Wasn't sure I'd make it. Where
you headed?*"

"*Pocatello.*"

*The rider raised his eyebrows.* "*I.F. might be
more realistic.*"

"*There is that. It close?*"

"*About there. I can talk you in.*"

"*If you can see the road tonight, you're not human.*"
*The man smiled.* "*Pull on out. Take it slow.*"

"*I'm a little low on gas, too.*"

*The man leaned over to check the fuel gauge.*
"*That's plenty.*"

*The tires spun as Portis tapped the accelerator. He
backed off, felt the rear end fishtail again before the car
eased forward.* "*You from around here, then?*"

"*I know it well enough. You want to bear slightly left
up here.*"

*They crept along, speedometer reading 10 miles per
hour. Portis nudged the wheel left, felt the car drift. He
glanced at his passenger.*

*"Just steer. I don't want to get stuck out here any more than you."* He fingered something in his shirt pocket, pointed ahead, directing Portis' attention back to the road. Portis nodded. *"Brian Portis,"* he said.

*"Ben Jenkins,"* the man said, as if to himself. He held his hands to the non-working heater vents, then rolled his eyes up to the shuddering canvas roof. *"Just visiting, then?"*

*"Sales run. Ragtop seemed great at the airport."*

The man nodded. *"Selling... ?"*

*"Crap."* Brian Portis shook his head. *"Loads and loads of crap. For oil wells. And no one buying. I just want to make the stop in Pocatello, then go home."*

*"New to it?"*

*" A 'promotion,' they called it. An 'opportunity.'"* Portis glanced at the man. Why was he telling him all this? Because it beats singing to yourself, he thought. *"Getting me off salary and on straight commission. Easing me out the door, truth be told."*

*"So why do it? You want to bear right – follow the hedge line there, you see it?"*

Brian Portis leaned toward what looked like a low, dark wall to his right. Why was he here, anyway? *"I'm fully-vested in three years. Too much to just throw away. With a family and all."*

The other man nodded. *"You don't sound too happy about that."*

*"Well, that's life, isn't it? You can't just do what you want."*

*"Why not?"*

239

"Did I mention my wife and kids?" As if a vagrant Granola-cruncher knew anything about responsibility.

"You happy?"

"They are. With food and a home and all their bills paid."

"How you gonna make them happy if you can't make yourself happy? Ease back to your left just a bit. There's a bridge – you see the guardrails?"

Portis looked at his passenger. The man had some nerve. And clueless. Then Portis felt the rear end start to float and the car slewed sideways, sliding broadside toward the cement railing.

Idiot! He had let the conversation distract him. Let an idiot distract him. The car continued its slow-motion slide. Let off on the gas, Portis thought, and don't even think of touching the brakes.

"Steer into it," the other man murmured.

"I am!" The left quarter-panel crunched against the cement. Portis felt the impact deep in his bowels. He had a quick glimpse of a dark stream roiling below, then the car lurched back to the right, toward the other guardrail.

"Steer into it," the man said louder. "It doesn't make sense, but do it!"

Shaking, Portis steered into the turn. After a long, slow second, the car straightened itself and nosed across the bridge onto solid ground.

"Like a pro," Jenkins said.

"Who are you?" Portis' hands were still shaking.

*And the man wouldn't shut up.*

*"Voice in the wilderness."*

*"Why should I listen to you?"*

*"Seems like you want to. Ease back to your right again, and you should start to see buildings. The road runs pretty straight from here."*

*Portis steered right and was pleased to see dark shapes – long, low buildings – materialize out of the darkness. He saw a streetlight, then another, and soon could make out the road without his headlights or Jenkins's help. He saw a gas station, but it was closed. Like everything else in Idaho, apparently.*

*"Anything open in this town?"*

*"Oh, sure, once we hit town-proper."*

*"Gas would be nice."*

*Jenkins looked at the fuel gauge again. "No worries. How about fuel for you?"*

*Portis just then noticed how hungry he was. His last food had been breakfast in Jackson that morning. A lifetime ago. Buildings grew taller, crowding the road, but all were dark. They looked like warehouses. The road sloped down and they passed below an overpass. Headlights approached. A police car, creeping in the opposite direction. Nothing else moved. Portis nodded. "Food would be good. Hot food."*

*"Hang a right up here," the other man said, pointing to a cross street between high, dark buildings. An alley, almost.*

Brian Portis glanced at him, skeptical again. What trust he had felt taking directions on the road was evaporating. A scruffy hitchhiker was asking him to turn down a dark side street in a strange town – 'D Street,' the sign said. Great, just great.

"There's food and gas. I promise."

The man had guided him to town, Portis thought. He slowed and started the turn, ready to spin the car on the icy road and chase the police car. Ahead, down D Street, Portis saw lights a block away. Windows of a restaurant, light spilling yellow onto the snow-covered road. Neon beer signs winked bright as he pulled closer, red, green, and pink. 'The Frosty Gator,' a painted sign said, showing a seated alligator wearing a ski cap, scarf and boots and holding an oversized beer mug. Portis had to laugh at the sight.

"You've got to be kidding me."

"Best burgers in town," Jenkins said. "My treat? For the ride?"

The best burger in town, in a warm restaurant, sounded better than anything else to Brian Portis just then. He guided the car to what looked like a curb and shut off the engine.

"There's gas up at your first left, and a couple decent hotels a few blocks straight ahead," Jenkins said. "Someone to fix that heater, too."

"I'll probably keep on to Pocatello."

"Your choice." Jenkins shrugged. "But here's as good as anywhere. Most places are pretty much the same. It's *who you are makes them good or bad. Worse places than Idaho Falls."*

*"Like where?"*

*"Inside your head right now. Inside your guts."* Jenkins stepped across the snow-drifted sidewalk and opened the Frosty Gator's door for Portis.

The warm air wrapped Portis like a thick blanket and pulled him in, washing away any anger at his passenger. More neon signs cluttered the walls, as did several TVs, all tuned to ESPN and CNN. He stood blinking for a moment until a waitress nodded them toward a booth. Jenkins ordered them two Irish coffees and walked to the restroom, leaving Portis to himself again.

National news blared from a TV over his head. He hadn't seen or heard the news in days. Yet here, in this random sports bar in this random town, on this strange night, that didn't seem to matter. He knew all the places mentioned, understood all the words the news anchors used, but he might have been watching the news in a foreign language, from places he'd never heard of.

Portis smiled. He would be headed home soon, back to Texas. Just a few more days. He imagined how Sally's and the girls' faces would look when he walked through the door. Yes, they would be happy. He laughed at himself, at his unreasoned anger. His passenger was right. He wasn't happy. He needed to change that. For all their sakes.

The waitress slid a clear glass of coffee in front of him, whipped cream mounded high. Portis could smell the *whiskey steaming up from the glass. He closed his eyes and took a long sip, letting the hot glass warm his hands.*

*"Ready to order?" The waitress smiled. She reminded him of someone. Someone from home.*

*"I'll wait for the other gentleman." Portis smiled back, finally relaxing.*

*"What gentleman?"*

*"The one I came in with. He ordered the drinks?"*

*"You... ordered one drink when you came in. Alone." Her brows creased.*

*Suspicion surged through Portis. He fumbled at his pocket until he felt his keys, his wallet. That was OK, then. "You saw no one come in with me?"*

*She shook her head. "You OK?"*

*Brian Portis excused himself and stepped back outside. The car was still there, grill and headlights indistinguishable and ragtop sagging under fresh snow falling heavier than ever. He glanced at the street and sidewalk, saw his own footprints mixed with dozens of others leading to the restaurant door, all filling in with the thick, wet snow.*

LaVergne, TN USA
21 March 2011

221057LV00001B/1/P